What Others Say About...

MW01248103

Decorating for Sundays and Holy Days
Cycles A, B, and C
by Bernadette Snyder and Hazelmai Terry

"Liturgists and catechists, take note of this practical resource for enhancing the Sunday and holy day liturgies in separate volumes for each of the three cycles. In addition to simple decorating suggestions, there are suggestions for parish celebrations and reflections."

The Catholic Standard

"Has your parish taken down its Christmas decorations yet? Does it decorate for religious occasions other than Christmas and Easter? Bernadette Snyder and Hazelmai Terry believe that every Sunday is a special occasion. In *Decorating for Sundays and Holy Days*, they suggest appropriate decor for every week of the year. If you're involved in your parish's liturgy preparation, you might want to check out these three books for each of the cycles."

Jim Breig
Bringing Religion Home

"The authors offer a wonderful resource book for every parish. Each book contains much more than decorating ideas for Sundays and holy days. In addition to their decorating ideas for the side altar, the book includes suggested celebrations and reflections for each Sunday. They obviously know how to make a Mass special and offer many beautiful and inspiring ideas that do not take too much time for any parish to use. This book would be a welcome asset to any parish."

Peggy Weber
The Observer

Decorations for 44 Parish Celebrations
by Bernadette Snyder and Hazelmai Terry

"Most parishes even in small towns could readily handle the kinds of decorations described in this simple, tasteful, well-written book. All advice about altar decorations, bulletin announcements, decor for parish parties, etc., is varied, appropriate, inexpensive, and worth the trouble."

Mississippi Today

THEMES
HOMILY SUGGESTIONS
ACTIVITIES

CYCLE B

DECORATING
For Sundays & Holy Days

Bernadette McCarver Snyder & Hazelmai McCarver Terry

TWENTY-THIRD PUBLICATIONS
Mystic, Connecticut

Twenty-Third Publications
185 Willow Street
P.O. Box 180
Mystic, CT 06355
(203) 536-2611

ISBN 0-89622-446-5
Library of Congress Catalog Card Number 88-72014

DEDICATION

We dedicate this book to our long-suffering husbands—Robert Terry and Bill Snyder—who have put up with baskets and bundles of Unidentified Liturgical Objects in the attic, pots and posies and posters stored in the garage, and liturgically "meaningful" centerpieces in the middle of Sunday dinner—which required reaching for the roast around rocks and sandpaper in Lent, saintly statues for feast days, and an Easter "promise" tree that dripped decorations into the gravy. To two good sports and two good husbands—with love from

Hazelmai and Bernadette

Contents

INTRODUCTION

This book is an invitation, an opportunity, and maybe even a challenge. The ideas in it are primarily for the parish Liturgy Committee but they could also be adapted by teachers planning celebrations for students or by parents trying to develop family activities and traditions.

The decorations, themes, activities, and reflections are meant to be used the way you would use a microscope or a spotlight or even a pointing finger: to draw attention! No one can improve on Scripture readings but maybe by pointing to them every Sunday, you can help the average parishioner notice them more and remember their messages. No one can improve on the Mass or make it more special than it already is, but perhaps you can help people rediscover its beauty and joy.

Suppose you had a special friend, someone you had seen again and again for years and years, someone important to you but so familiar that you thought there could be no surprises. And then one day, that friend said or did something totally unexpected and caught your attention enough to make you look more closely and consider more deeply and perhaps love more dearly. That's the kind of result an unusual decoration or parish activity could accomplish.

Some years ago, children were taught that they should learn to know God, love God, and serve God. Today, many people still strive for that, ever reaching toward new dimensions of understanding, a new awareness of shared love, and a surer sense of how and where to show up or sign up for service. But sometimes we all get lazy and complacent and stop noticing and reaching. That's when we need something to get our attention.

In a world where traffic sounds drown the song of the thrush and deadlines steal the time for a walk in the woods or a game with the children, it's all too easy to hurry to Mass on Sunday and wait nervously for the familiar prayers to end so we can scurry off to some other activity and miss out on the special Scripture message of the day, miss out on the opportunity to know, love, and serve.

The document, "Environment and Art in Catholic Worship,"

issued by the Bishops' Committee on the Liturgy, reminds us that "God does not need liturgy; people do, and people have only their own arts and styles of expression with which to celebrate."

That's what this book suggests: using your own art and style of expression. Decorations do not always have to be fancy or formal or exotic or an expensive arrangement from the florist. Jesus used ordinary, everyday examples when he preached in parables. He used things familiar to the people of his day and his time. You can follow his lead—as we should always do—and use ordinary things to decorate the altar and draw attention to the readings, the teachings. You can use things familiar to the people of this day and this time.

Although the traditional white cloths, golden candelabra, and formal flower arrangements are always beautiful, something a bit different or unusual might be just unexpected enough to get the attention of the person in the pew.

That's why this book is an invitation and an opportunity. It invites you to use your imagination and look for new ways to focus attention on the important Scripture message of the day. It suggests possible decorations but only as idea-triggers to help you see new possibilities for decorations, parish activities, and reflections. And perhaps it challenges you to look around and be aware of the infinite variety of God's creations and then to put some of that variety into your liturgical celebrations.

How to Use This Book

As in our earlier books for Cycle A and Cycle C, each Sunday or Holy Day is set up in simple sections: *Inspiration:* A brief selection from the readings of the day that suggested a decoration theme to us. Perhaps the readings will suggest to you an entirely different theme or a variation on the one we chose. *Decoration:* Possibilities for carrying out the theme with a decoration in front of or near the altar, plus extras that might be placed in other areas of the church. *Celebration:* A parish activity that can be planned to tie in with and further emphasize the theme of the day. *Reflection:* A thought that could be read before Mass, or printed (in whole or in part) in the bulletin, or used as a springboard for the homily.

Some things to consider in using this book: *Be alert:* Always make sure that the decorations are not so overwhelming that they detract from the liturgy. When in doubt, use less instead of adding more. *Be inventive:* Find a small table or bench or something that is just the right size and height to fit in front of and below the altar in your church. Use this as a base or platform where you can display decorations to be a focal point and yet not be as prominent as the altar itself. *Be creative:* Sometimes place decorations behind the altar or on side altars or on the walls, down the aisle, hanging from the ceiling, at the back door or in the vestibule. *Be prayerful:* Look before you leap and pray before you plan. Ask for guidance so that you can create a memorable decoration but more importantly, a prayerful environment.

Note: This book is one of three that suggest decorating and celebrating ideas for the Scripture readings in Year A, Year B, and Year C. Decorations for seasonal days like Mother's Day, Labor Day, etc., can be found in another book, *Decorations for 44 Parish Celebrations.* All are available from Twenty-Third Publications.

First Sunday of Advent

Isaiah 63:16-17, 19; 64:2-7
1 Corinthians 1:3-9
Mark 13:33-37

"O Lord, you are our father; we are the clay and you are the potter; we are all the work of your hands."

Decoration

In addition to the traditional Advent wreath today, use a draping of burlap or some straw mats to form the background for a display of clay pots, bowls, pitchers, etc. Intersperse with greenery. If you know someone who works with ceramics, perhaps you could borrow a potter's wheel or unfinished greenware or partially decorated, unfinished ceramic pieces to include with the finished ones. You might even add some stick figures or animals made by children of play dough—anything you have available that would convey the idea of working with clay.

Addition

To herald this first week of Advent, make flags instead of banners! Attach them to the side walls of the church so they will jut out from the wall, calling attention to the upcoming four weeks of Advent. Make three flags of purple and one of pink for each side wall. Or make all the flags one color: the rich, deep blue that is currently being used by some liturgists to signify Advent. If the design of your church would preclude the flags, make banners using the design of clay pots. Or hang a mobile made with various shapes of clay pots.

Celebration

Ask one of the parish clubs to sponsor a Christmas sale after all Masses, offering Advent wreaths and Advent books in addition to Catholic books and religious articles that would be appropriate for Christmas gifts or stocking-stuffers for both children and adults. Or announce that for the next four weeks, there will be an insert in the bulletin (or a flyer in the pews or at the church doors) that will include family ideas for Advent Adventures.

Meditation

Today's altar decorations reflect the message in the first reading, "O Lord, you are our Father; we are the clay and you are the potter; we are all the work of your hands." Just as God has shaped us, we too often help shape the lives of our children, friends, relatives, co-workers. In this "do your own thing" age, perhaps we've forgotten about the importance of giving a good example. If strangers judged you only by what they saw, only by the way they saw you live your daily life, would they immediately know you are a Catholic, a Christian? If strangers judged you only by the way you celebrate Christmas, would they immediately know you are celebrating Jesus' birthday?

To help you set a good example by "keeping Christ in Christmas," we are having a sale in the vestibule today of Advent wreaths, Advent meditation books, and Christ-centered items appropriate as Christmas gifts or stocking-stuffers for both children and adults. We also invite you to take home one of the Advent Adventure flyers, which suggests ideas to help you and your family turn Advent into an adventure.

ADVENT ADVENTURE
Family Project #1

To celebrate this "waiting" time before Christmas, _____ parish invites you to embark on an Advent Adventure by spending a few minutes each week of Advent for a little family project.

 Start this first week of Advent by making a family Advent prayer card. Simply cut around the heavy outlines, then fold on the dotted lines. Cut a slit on the broken line and insert the tab. (If this is not sturdy enough, paste it on a heavier paper.) Put this card on the dinner table or in a prominent place (on the TV?).

Now get out your family Advent wreath (where did you pack it away last year?) or make a new one. All you need is a circle of greenery with four candles—one pink and three purple.

 Each night of Advent, before dinner or whenever the family is together, say the Advent prayer on your card and add family petitions. The first week, light one candle. The next week, light the second… Discuss the week's theme.

The Advent wreath prayers may be a long-time custom in your family but this year, you won't have to wonder what prayers to say because your Advent Prayer Card will be right on your table (or TV!).

Watch the bulletin next Sunday for another Advent Adventure—Family Project #2.

Flyer for 1st week of Advent—print on both sides of colored paper. Side 1.

ADVENT

PRAYER FOR 1ST WEEK

*Theme of week—Anticipation

Dear Lord, thank you for this first week
of anticipation—of waiting for Christmas.
Bless us as we gather together in your
name, Oh Lord, to share, to grow and to
love. Help us to make this Advent a time
to prepare more than we ever have before
for the coming of Emmanuel. Amen.

PRAYER FOR 2ND WEEK

*Theme of week—Hope, concern for others

Dear Lord, fill our hearts with hope,
our minds with concern for others.
Make us more open to each other and let
us reach out to share problems as well
as happiness. Bless all those who are
lonely or unloved this holy season. Amen.

3RD WEEK *Theme of week—Joy, light

Dear Jesus, Light of the World,
Shine above me, below me, around me.
Dear Jesus, Light of the World,
Take me, mold me, use me, hold me. Amen.

4TH WEEK *Theme of week—Acceptance

Oh God, thank you for the many gifts you
have given us. Help us to appreciate our
blessings and share them with others as we
prepare to celebrate Jesus' birthday. Amen.

SECOND SUNDAY OF ADVENT

Isaiah 40:1-5, 9-11
2 Peter 3, 8-14
Mark 1:1-8

*" 'I send my messenger before you to prepare your way....
Make ready the way of the Lord....' Thus it was that John the
Baptizer appeared in the desert proclaiming a baptism of re-
pentance."*

Decoration

In addition to the Advent wreath and flags from last week,
make an arrangement to illustrate John the Baptizer. Possibly use
a fake-fur fabric to depict the camel's haircloth. Add a rough
leather belt or strip of leather, sandals with straps loosened and
perhaps a rough stick or branch to resemble a walking stick.
Also include a clear jar of honey and some sprays of greenery or
a shock of dried grasses to illustrate the desert.

Celebration

Although this is a busy season, you might plan a pancake
breakfast and serve the pancakes with honey. Or you might ask
a local beekeeper to provide small jars of honey for sale after
Mass. Or you could have a parishioner dress to appear like John
the Baptizer, wearing sandals and a rough, loose garment tied
with a leather belt, and carrying a rugged walking stick. He
could come in with the entrance procession or with the offertory
procession. He could even do the readings today. In addition,
you will provide the Advent Adventure flyers for families to
take home this second week.

Reflection

Today's gospel reminds us of the words of Isaiah, "Make
ready the way of the Lord." And it tells us of John the Baptizer
who proclaimed the coming of "one more powerful than I ...who
will baptize you in the Holy Spirit." Our altar decoration is a reminder of the brave man who raised his voice in the desert, the
man who wore camel's hair and ate wild honey. It challenges us
to do as he did—to make ready the way of the Lord—as we

spend these waiting weeks before Christmas. It also challenges us to become proclaimers, to spread the good news of Jesus and to invite others to share with us in a holy and reverent celebration of the Advent season. Please take home a copy of this week's Advent Adventure suggestions and use the ideas with your family during the this second week of Advent as we make ready the way and prepare for the coming.

ADVENT ADVENTURE
Family Project #2—A Christmas Surprise!

Did you know that during Advent, we celebrate a very special and appropriate feast day? On December 6, we celebrate the feast of St. Nicholas!

Legend tells us that St. Nicholas once heard about three sisters who couldn't get married because their parents were too poor to provide the dowry that was traditional at that time, so St. Nicholas decided to surprise them. One night, he left three small bags of gold at their house and in the morning, they were happily surprised to find such wonderful gifts. Today, in some countries, children leave shoes (instead of socks!) outside their bedroom doors on the night of December 5 and the next morning, on St. Nicholas's day, they find the shoes full of candy and toys.

So how about having a St. Nick celebration at your house? One night this week, gather the family together and ask each to share a story about the best surprise gift ever received. Then plan to give a surprise St. Nicholas gift to someone else this Advent.

Perhaps you could bake cookies together, then give packages of them to someone who would never expect to get a gift from your family. Or you could invite an elderly friend or shut-in to go with your family for an Advent outing to attend a Christmas pageant or visit one of the beautiful outdoor Christmas nativity scenes in the area.

Flyer for 2nd week of Advent—Side 1.

Or each member of the family could think of some small gift personally wished for, then buy it, wrap it and give it to someone else! Or make home-made Christmas cards together and send them to out-of-town relatives or to anyone who would be surprised to receive a card from your family.

Or plan to adopt a poor family. Ask your pastor if he knows of some family who could use some extra help this year. Set aside a time when you can all go as a family to choose a gift (or gifts) for them. Wrap the gift(s) in pretty paper and then make it personal by enclosing a family letter. Either write a letter together or ask each family member to write a Christmas note (even the smallest child can draw a picture to be included) to make the gift less like charity and more like a friend-to-friend gift.

In this second week of Advent, use these ideas or your own to plan a family surprise for someone else and share a happy Advent Adventure.

THIRD SUNDAY OF ADVENT

Isaiah 61:1-2, 10-11
1 Thessalonians 5:16-24
John 1:6-8, 19-28

"As the earth brings forth its plants...so will the Lord God make justice and praise spring up before all nations."

Decoration

Since today's gospel reading again speaks of John the Baptizer, you could retain the decoration from last week. Or, if your parish is planning to collect gifts or food for another parish, you could simply make a bank of Christmas greenery, branches of evergreens, or green plants in front of the altar and put some of the gift-wrapped boxes of gifts or food items amidst the greenery.

Celebration

This week you can make an announcement about the parish plan for helping others, outlining details. Or, if there is no parish plan for a Christmas charity this year, check into local groups that are collecting food or gifts and announce where parishioners can go to make individual donations. Also remind parishioners to take home the Advent Adventure flyer for week 3.

Reflection

Our altar decoration today reminds us of several points in today's readings. In the first reading, we hear that "As the earth brings forth its plants, so will the Lord God make justice and praise spring up." In the second reading, we are reminded to "never cease praying, to render constant thanks." And in the gospel, we again see John the Baptizer who "came as a witness to testify to the light." In this season of Advent, we are challenged to follow all these: to seek justice, to say thanks and to witness to the light. The obvious way to do all these things in this holy season is by sharing our blessings with others who are less fortunate. No matter how poor we are or how frugal we must be in our Christmas celebrations, there are those who are more needy than we. In justice, we can find some way to share with them, some way to give thanks to the Lord for our blessings, some way to witness and testify to the light of Christ. Share yourself this Christmas with others—give gifts of cash or food to the poor or give a gift of time by volunteering to spend a few hours at a soup kitchen or a charity that will need help in serving Christmas dinners to the needy or invite someone lonely to share your own family's Christmas celebrations. What better Christmas gift for the child Jesus than an act of justice, thanks, and witness.

We remind you to take home this third week's Advent Adventure and use the ideas to become Advent Angels.

ADVENT ADVENTURE
Family Project #3—Advent Angels, Secrets and Surprises

Last week, you embarked on an adventure to surprise someone outside your own family. This week it's time for inside the family secrets and surprises!

Invite every member of the family to become an Advent Angel! Gather all the family together one night and share a snack. Then write down the name of each person on a slip of paper and put all the slips into a bowl or basket. Each family member can draw a name (self-named slips should be put back for another drawing.) No one should tell whose name was drawn—it's a secret!

During this week, you will each become an Advent Angel to the person whose name you drew. Once each day—or at least, several times during the week—be an angel by secretly doing something nice for that person.

To get started, you might make up a list of possible angel projects and keep the list on the refrigerator door as a helpful reminder during the week.

Here are a few Advent Angel ideas for secrets and surprises:

Do someone else's usual chore
Take out the trash
Wash the windows on the family car
Make the beds
Clean up the bathroom
Say a prayer or light a candle for someone and then write an anonymous note to tell him or her about it
Pick up toys without being told
Pick up someone else's clothes off the floor and hang them up or put them in the laundry
Fold the clean laundry
Rake leaves or shovel snow
Water house plants
Write an anonymous note explaining "Why I like you" or "Why you are special" or "Why I love you."

Your family may think of a lot of other angel ideas and maybe this "secret mission" could become a yearly family tradition.

Watch the bulletin next week for the last Advent Adventure.

Fourth Sunday of Advent

2 Samuel 7:1-5, 8-11, 16
Romans 16:25-27
Luke 1:26-38

"The angel Gabriel was sent from God...to a virgin... the virgin's name was Mary...Mary said, "I am the maidservant of the Lord."

Decoration
Since you will be getting out the Nativity scene in preparation for Christmas, use the statue of the angel—or some other angel statue—as the focus of today's decoration. Use a white cloth for the background and surround the statue with white flowers or greenery interspersed with lots of white vigil lights.

Addition
You could add two banners: one, a side-view silhouette of the pregnant Mary, with arms upraised in praise; the second, a silhouette of a kneeling Joseph with head bowed in prayer and acceptance.

Celebration
Although this is a busy time of year, perhaps you could plan a simple parish celebration for one evening. Issue an invitation for everyone to gather in the parish hall for an evening of carols. As they arrive, serve warm cider or cold punch and cookies. After everyone has gathered, have someone come in dressed as an angel, followed by the choir singing, "It Came Upon a Midnight Clear." At the end of the song, the angel should invite all to "Follow me now to Bethlehem." All should now process to the main entrance of the church. As they enter, the church should be in semi-darkness with only candlelight if possible. (You might pass out candles to each person approaching the church door.) Inside the church, a Christmas "surprise" will be waiting—in front of the altar, a living Nativity scene. (Arrange to have parishioners dressed as Mary, Joseph, the Shepherds...all positioned by a crib.) Everyone else can now gather around and join the choir in

singing a selection of Christmas carols. At the end of the carols, the lights can be turned on all at once and those in the living scene can rise and mingle with their friends. Perhaps you might like to have some children dressed as angels who will stand at the door and pass out some inexpensive mementos—small ornaments or holy cards—as people leave the church.

Reflection

Our altar decoration today echoes the gospel reading which tells of the Angel Gabriel coming to Mary. Mary is deeply troubled—as we all are when we are asked to do something that seems beyond our capabilities. Mary wondered what the greeting meant just as we all often wonder about the things God asks us to do. Mary asks, "How can this be?"—a question we all often ask God. But Mary does not let the worry or the wonder stop her. She freely says, "I am the maidservant of the Lord. Let it be done to me as you say." This week, reflect on Mary's answer. Ask yourself if you are as generous as she was, if you are willing to be a servant of the Lord, without question. Ask Mary to draw you closer to her son in this last week of waiting for his coming.

We remind you once again to take home this week's Advent Adventure—the final one of this Advent season.

ADVENT

Adventure Family Project #4

The theme of the fourth week in Advent is acceptance and the last candle is lighted on the Advent wreath. This week would be the perfect time for a joyous candle-lit family celebration.

One evening, make it a family project to put up your Christmas crib scene. If you don't have one, make it a family outing to shop for one (there are many lovely ones available at this time of year, even inexpensive cardboard ones). When the crib is in place, plan to have a candlelight crib procession the next evening.

Gather in the room farthest from the crib and turn out all the lights in the house. Mom or Dad or an older child can carry a lighted candle and light the way as you "process" to the crib. You might like to sing "Silent Night" or some appropriate hymn. Kneel at the crib and read the gospel account of the first Christmas (Luke 2: 15-20) or say this prayer:

"Dear Jesus, bless this crib that we have set up in memory of your birth. Help us to remember each time we look at it that you came down to us at Bethlehem because you loved us. Remind us too that the presents we give and receive are given and received in memory of your love. Bless our family and our world with peace and joy. Amen."

Now "process" to the kitchen to have an early birthday party for Jesus! Use the leader's candle to light the candles on a birthday cake (which you have made or bought and decorated with the words, "Happy Birthday, Jesus"). Sing the birthday song together, blow out the candles, turn on the lights, and have a happy party! You might include balloons or party favors, milk or punch, games or stories. Talk about the first Christmas and what you think it might have been like, how Mary and Joseph looked or felt. Discuss what you could do as a family to give Jesus a birthday present.

One last adventure! On Christmas Eve, try to have most of the chores done early so you can find time to gather the family by the Christmas tree to say a little Christmas prayer together. You might use this one:

"Dear Lord, the evergreen branches of this tree are symbols of your everlasting light; the sparkling lights and decorations, reflections of your presence; the gifts beneath it, reminders of your many gifts to us. Help us to keep the peace and joy of Christmas in our hearts all through the year. Amen. "

CHRISTMAS
(At Midnight)

Isaiah 9:1-6
Titus 2:11-14
Luke 2:1-14

"She gave birth to her first-born son and wrapped him in swaddling clothes and laid him in a manger."

Decoration

What could be better than the traditional Nativity Scene, swags of greenery, poinsettias, sparkling lights, and Christmas trees? People would be disappointed if you didn't include at least some of these. But it's always interesting to add a few variations. Flank the scene with Christmas trees trimmed all in crystal—strands of crystal beads, clear glass ornaments, silver icicles and lots of clear white twinkling lights. Or, if you plan a children's Mass, how about a Christmas tree trimmed in holy cards, the kind children love, the kind that have pictures of saints and gold trim and fancy designs (religious goods' stores still have a big variety of these.) At the end of Mass, the celebrant could invite all the children to come up to the tree and choose a holy card to take home. Or invite all parishioners to bring one special ornament to add to the parish tree. Before Mass, while carols are being sung, people could come up and trim the tree with their ornaments. (You could have two helpers stationed on ladders to add ornaments to upper branches.) All these ornaments could be saved, with more added each year until you have a unique parish memory tree.

Addition

If you have used the purple or blue flags on the side walls during Advent, replace them now with brighter flags. Use gold, silver, white with gold trim or whatever colors would coordinate with your other decorations. Or make one large banner to hang behind the altar or two for each side, using the design of a "Happy Birthday, Jesus" cake and other birthday trimmings like confetti, balloons, etc. Again, use colors that coordinate with the other decorations and possibly glue on sequins, curly ribbons, etc.

Celebration

When people arrive for Mass, have the crib scene assembled—except for the baby Jesus. While soft music plays to announce the entrance procession, have candle bearers come in first, then possibly small children carrying gaily-wrapped gift boxes, then other children ringing small bells and finally, the celebrant carrying a statue of the baby Jesus. As the celebrant places the statue in the Nativity Scene, all parishioners could join in singing, "Happy birthday, dear Jesus."

Reflection

The popular comicstrip that features a baby named Marvin once showed the baby saying, "Let me get this straight. Christmas is Jesus' birthday. But I get all the presents. Is this a great religion or what!" Well, this is a great religion but we all seem to concentrate on worldly gifts and overlook the fact that Jesus is the one who first gave us a present on his birthday. On that first Christmas, he came into the world as a lowly babe to bring us the gift of salvation. Let us give thanks; let us rejoice; let us resolve anew to get to know Jesus better so that we can love him more and serve him faithfully in this world and be happy with him forever in the next.

SUNDAY AFTER CHRISTMAS
Holy Family

Sirach 3:2-6, 12-14
Colossians 3:12-21
Luke 2:22-40 or 2:22, 39-40

"They came to offer in sacrifice a pair of turtledoves or two young pigeons, in accord with the dictate in the law of the Lord."

Decoration
The Nativity Scene will still be in place today, appropriately drawing all eyes to the holy family on this, the Sunday we celebrate them.

Addition
Make two banners: one with the design of two turtle doves, another with a heart pierced by a sword. Or letter signs with the "titles" of various family members—mother, father, cousin, niece, uncle, grandmother.... Hang these at various places about the church—possibly along the side walls or at the ends of pews—to remind all that this is a family Sunday.

Celebration
Since this is a holiday time with schools closed and some people on vacation, why not have a free Sunday afternoon at the movies for parish families! Although many movies today are non-family, there are still a few good G-rated ones available at the video stores, so rent one! Borrow a large-screen television or several smaller ones and set up folding chairs for the audience. Sell popcorn at a dime a bag and have some cold drinks on hand. Invite families to bring along extended-family members: cousins, grandparents.... And enjoy a relaxing, wholesome afternoon.

Reflection
Today's reading reminds us once again that Joseph and Mary always followed the Law. They knew their son was the Messiah but they still took him to the Temple and made a sacrifice in accordance with the dictate of the Law. Today's families are not

always so careful about obeying the laws of their church. So the next time you are tempted to bend the law a little to make your life a bit more convenient, think about Mary and Joseph. Would they have done that? Would Jesus do that? Our decorations today remind us that the holy family of Jesus, Mary and Joseph had other relatives too. They had an extended family as most do: Mary's parents, Ann and Joachim, her cousin Elizabeth, Jesus' cousin, John the Baptizer, and others mentioned in Scripture. To honor all our family members, we invite you to bring them along this afternoon to a free Sunday afternoon movie! The movie, _____, will be shown at ____P.M. in the parish hall and there will be soft drinks and popcorn or you can bring your own snacks. But be sure to bring along the whole family so you can celebrate together this Holy Family Sunday.

JANUARY 1
Solemnity of Mary, Mother of God

Numbers 6:22-27
Galatians 4:4-7
Luke 2:16-21

"The Lord bless you and keep you! The Lord look upon you kindly and give you peace."

Decoration
Although the Christmas decorations will still be in place today, you will want to call attention to Mary on this special feast, so how about rounding up all sorts of candlesticks and candles of various sizes, shapes, heights. Just fill the side altar in front of Mary's statue with lighted candles as a shining tribute. With all the Christmas decorations in place, you will not need additional flowers but you could add a bit of trailing ivy or other greenery to complete the arrangement.

Celebration
This is the day when many churches give out calendars for the new year. If yours does, you can call attention to that. And you might like to start the custom of distributing a parish calendar-of-the month. Some parishes print this on the front of their bulletin at the first of each month. Others distribute it as a flyer or bulletin insert. On the calendar you can note all the upcoming church activities for that month so that parishioners can post the calendar on a refrigerator or family bulletin board as a reminder. You can also add a few spiritual suggestions to some calendar days: "Say a prayer for the pastor and all priests." "Visit or call a neighbor you haven't seen for a while." "Spend time with someone in the family who needs a little extra attention." "Take a quiet walk and give God a chance to talk to you."

Reflection
In today's first reading, we hear the comforting words—"the Lord bless and keep you...the Lord look upon you kindly and give you peace." As we enter a new year, everyone longs for

peace—in the world, in our families, and in our individual lives and hearts. And today we look to the queen of peace—to Mary—as we celebrate this feast of the Solemnity of Mary. We have many lighted candles by her statue to remind us all to go to her in this new year and ask her to help us find peace and acceptance.

We invite you to take home a calendar today and use it to mark the days of the New Year. We suggest that when you hang up the new calendar, you take last year's calendar and tear out the pages and literally crush and crumple each page and throw them in a bin for eventual recycling—as a symbol of getting rid of the old year and starting the new. Throw out all the frustrations and disappointments of last year and enter the new year with confidence, asking Mary and her son to look upon you kindly and give you peace.

EPIPHANY

Isaiah 60:1-6
Ephesians 3:2-3, 5-6
Matthew 2:1-12

"After Jesus' birth in Bethlehem of Judea during the reign of King Herod, astrologers from the east arrived....The star...went ahead of them until it came to a standstill over the place where the child was."

Decoration

The Christmas decorations will continue in place for the last Sunday. You will need only to supply decorated boxes or baskets or some kind of containers for the chalk to be used in today's celebration. You might cover the boxes with gold paper to look like the gifts of gold of the Wise Men.

Celebration

Let the entrance procession begin today with candles and incense and joyful music. Ask members of the liturgy committee or greeters or school children to process in, carrying boxes or baskets filled with pieces of chalk (enough to give each person a piece to take home.) Ask the celebrant to bless the chalk before Mass. At the end of Mass, those who processed in with the chalk should stand at the church doors and distribute it to parishioners as they leave.

Reflection

Today's readings tell us that "the glory of the Lord shines upon you" and you are "sharers of the promise." The gospel recounts the journey of the Wise Men following a star to find the light of the Messiah, the redeemer of the world, the glory and the promise of salvation. Today, we invite you to celebrate this journey and this light by having your own Epiphany journey, a custom that is practiced by people in many parts of the world on or near the feast of the Epiphany. At the beginning of Mass, the celebrant blessed pieces of chalk and we invite you each to take home a piece of this blessed chalk. Alone, or with your family, go to the front door of your house and say a prayer, asking God to bless you and your family in the coming year. Then use the chalk to write over your doorpost "19 + C + M + B + 91" (to symbolize Caspar and Melchior and Balthasar and the year 1991, or whatever year you are beginning.) After you write that, say this little prayer, "As the brilliant light of the star led the Wise Men to find the newborn King, the Messiah, the redeemer, may the example of those Wise Men who journeyed afar—Caspar and Melchior and Balthasar—guide us and lead us on our spiritual journey in this year of Our Lord 1991."

SUNDAY AFTER EPIPHANY
Baptism of the Lord

Isaiah 42:1-4, 6-7
Acts 10:34-38
Mark 1:7-11

"Immediately on coming up out of the water, he saw the sky rent in two and the Spirit descending on him like a dove."

Decoration
Use a lace curtain or some lace material to make a pretty, scalloped swag across the front of the altar. At the center of the altar, attach one white dove. You can probably find one at a florist or craft store or silk flower shop. Or make one out of white cardboard or paper or use a ceramic dove. Behind the altar, hang two banners made of pale blue material with the design of a white cloud split in half: one half of the cloud on the left banner and the other half on the right banner.

Celebration
Have an instant-print shop make copies of the prayer "Come, Holy Spirit" and distribute these after Mass.

Reflection
Our altar decoration reflects the words of today's gospel: "He saw the sky rent in two and the Spirit descending on him like a dove." To honor the Spirit, we have printed copies of the prayer, "Come, Holy Spirit," which will be available after Mass at all the church doors. Take home one of these prayers and try to find a few minutes each day this week to really meditate on the words of this beautiful intercession. "Come, Holy Spirit. Fill the hearts of thy faithful. Enkindle in them the fire of thy divine love. Send forth thy Spirit. And they will be created and thou shalt renew the face of the earth."

Second Sunday in Ordinary Time

1 Samuel 3:3-10
1 Corinthians 6:13-15
John 1:35-42

"Samuel was sleeping in the temple of the Lord... The Lord called to Samuel, who answered, "Here I am."

Decoration
Make a small pallet in front of the altar, using a colorful quilt or blanket and a pillow. You might want to flank this with two tall plants or you could set a very low table by the pallet and add items that might be on Samuel's bedside table: a candle, a plant or bowl of fruit, a drinking glass, and small pitcher of water.

Celebration
Invite a guest speaker today to address the subject of religious vocations: the need for today's Catholics to again appreciate and applaud the special calling of a religious vocation, the need to encourage young people to accept the call to service of the Lord, the need for adults to show more respect for the work of the clergy, the need for families to point out to their children the many advantages and opportunities in the career of a priest or nun, and the need also for today's laity to volunteer to become lay ministers and to serve the parish in whatever capacity their talents allow.

Reflection
In today's reading, God called and Samuel answered. He didn't say, "Wait a minute" or "I'm sleeping now." He said, "Here I am Lord." When God calls you, do you immediately answer "Here I am Lord" or do you pretend to not hear the call? As God's people, we should always be on the watch, expectant, waiting to see God everywhere and to hear his call. Have you ever been to an airport and watched people waiting for a plane's arrival? They look eagerly at every new person who comes through the gate, tiptoeing to see better, alert, watchful, careful to not miss the one they're waiting to greet. That's the way we

should be: looking eagerly, watching for every sign of God's presence in our world, listening for every call. Have we been sleeping when we should have been alert? Have we been too busy to see, to hear, to recognize God's blessings? Too self-centered to feel the deep need for God's presence? Too unaware to notice God's hand reaching out to us? This week, stop...look...listen...watch...and welcome.

THIRD SUNDAY IN ORDINARY TIME

Jonah 3:1-51
Corinthians 7:29-31
Mark 1:14-20

"Come after me...."

Decoration
How about a decoration of newspapers day? Take several pages of the classified section and letter across the top in large bold letters, HELP WANTED. Arrange the papers in front of the altar so that this heading can be seen easily. Possibly add greenery on each side.

Celebration
If you have an evangelization committee in your parish, this would be a good day to ask people to volunteer to help. If you don't have one, it would be a good time to set up one. Perhaps one of the activities of this committee could be to put together an information letter to be mailed out to all non-Catholic residents of the area. In it, you could give a brief explanation of the Catholic faith and outline the various activities of your parish: study clubs, Bible study groups, convert preparation seminars, Knights of Columbus, Ladies Sodality, parish school, or parish school of religion program, widows' and widowers' group, senior citizen group, any out-reach program that helps the poor or visits nursing homes.... In the letter, issue an invitation to Mass (listing the various Mass times) or to any of the meetings. Include the name and address of a parishioner who would be happy to pick up the prospects and bring them to a parish gathering and/or give them further information about the Catholic faith.

Reflection
In today's first reading, the Lord told Jonah to take a message to Nineveh and Jonah went "according to the Lord's bidding." And in the gospel, Jesus tells fishermen, "Come after me," and they immediately abandon their nets and follow him. Our altar decoration reminds us all that help is still wanted. The Lord still

needs helpers to carry his message, to follow him and spread the good news. How could you help? Do you know of someone who has forgotten the message, who is no longer practicing the faith? Do you know of someone who might like to learn more about the Catholic religion but is just waiting for someone to invite them in? What could you do to help? Become an active member of our evangelization team (help us form a parish evangelization team) and share your faith by telling others of its richness. Look in today's bulletin for information about the parish evangelization committee.

FOURTH SUNDAY IN ORDINARY TIME

Deuteronomy 18:15-20
1 Corinthians 7:32-35
Mark 1:21-28

"I should like you to be free of all worries."

Decoration
Today make the focus of the decoration a large banner. On it, use the outline of a beaker—the narrow-necked glass container used in laboratories. Above the beaker have two strips of fabric or ribbon—one blue, one yellow—coming into the beaker as though you are pouring a liquid into it. Once inside the outline of the beaker, cross the strips over each other as though the two are mingling and then have the contents of the beaker made of a green fabric as though the blue and yellow have combined to create green. The banner would be enough decoration but you could add an arrangement of greenery in front of the altar with several laboratory beakers and fill them with water that has been dyed with food dye to look like blue, yellow, and green potions. (You could borrow the beakers from a high school lab or ask a science teacher to tell you where you could buy some inexpensive beakers.)

Celebration
Since everyone today seems worried about something and under stress, how about inviting a speaker to come and give a full-day seminar on stress? There are many good programs available and perhaps the parish could pay a qualified speaker to do this and treat parishioners to some good solid advice about how to cope. Or if the parish can't afford this, then charge an amount that would cover the expenses. Have it on Saturday so working people can attend and ask them to bring a brown bag lunch. Or have it in the evening and break up into two sessions on different evenings. This will depend on the speaker you find but it should be more than just one talk on one evening. Really arrange a worthwhile program.

Reflection

Today's first reading mentions false prophets; the second speaks of worries and the world's demands; and the gospel tells of a man with an unclean spirit. In today's society, we are beset on all sides with false prophets, demands of the world, and unclean spirits. We are all different and have different worries but, as our decoration depicts, two very different liquids can be poured into a beaker and mingle to make one new substance. So too we come together to form one body of Christ, one family of God. This week, try to put aside some of those worldly worries and spend a few minutes each day in quiet, restful prayer, celebrating and giving thanks for your membership in the body of Christ, the family of God.

(Since today's world does present us all with stress and worry, we have arranged to have a parish seminar to address the problem of stress. See today's bulletin for information and be sure to register for this helpful program.)

FIFTH SUNDAY IN ORDINARY TIME

Job 7:1-4, 6-7
1 Corinthians 9:16-19, 22-23
Mark 1:29-39

"...they brought him all who were ill and those possessed by demons..."

Decoration
Since today's readings seem to focus on problems and rainy days, make a decoration using umbrellas! Use those large decorated paper Chinese umbrellas, or pretty, real umbrellas. Open some in front of the altar or make a bank of greenery and lean some partially-opened umbrellas against that. Or make a mobile with the design of small umbrellas and hang it from the ceiling.

Celebration
Make up a flyer to pass out today, headed: GOOD SAMARITAN—HELPING HANDS. Inside, list various ways someone could offer emergency help to others in the parish. Find two or more people who could coordinate this and list their names and phone numbers in the flyer. Use information similar to this:

We invite all parishioners—young or old or in-between—to join in a Good Samaritan program. Please check where and how you could help or how you need help. Add your name and phone number and return to the rectory OR call one of the coordinators listed.
How can I be useful?
I can ___ give rides to school children ___ in the morning ___ in the afternoon.
I can ___ make a casserole for a family in an emergency situation;
___ go to a family home to help prepare a meal;
___ go to a family home to help care for children in an emergency situation;
___ care for children for a limited time in my home when there is a family crisis;
___ visit a new mother and help provide limited care for her and the baby;

___ visit someone recovering at home or in a hospital or nursing home;

___ run errands or do simple home chores for some elderly people or for someone who is ill;

___ help prepare a meal for an after-funeral family lunch.

Captains needed too! Would you be willing to offer your phone number as the contact person for your neighborhood for anyone who needs or can give help? ___

Name_____ Phone_____

If you need help right now or wish more information about giving help, call a coordinator today. Tell your friends, relatives, and neighbors about this program and encourage them to become Good Samaritans too. Please. There are people in your parish family who need you.

Reflection

In today's gospel, many people came to Jesus for help, people who were sick or possessed by demons. Our decoration reflects the fact that we all have rainy days occasionally, times when we are sick or possessed by the demons of trouble and worry. Right now there are parishioners who need a little help to get over a temporary problem, and there are parishioners who could provide that help. Please take home one of the Good Samaritan flyers in the pews today. Please let someone know when you need help or can give help. That's the way a family works!

First Sunday of Lent

Genesis 9:8-15
1 Peter 3:18-22
Mark 1:12-15

"He stayed in the wasteland forty days, put to the test there by Satan. He was with the wild beasts and angels waited on him."

Decoration

You may wish to establish one theme for Lent and stay with it every Sunday. You could put an arrangement of 40 jagged rocks in front of the altar intermingled with purple vigil lights and perhaps centered with a bowl of ashes from the Ash Wednesday service. Or, to reflect the desert, put some kind of plastic cloth on the floor (that will be easy to gather up) and put a deep layer of sand on it. Or use a piece of beige burlap to simulate sand. Add pieces of driftwood, large rocks, cactus.... And possibly a brass container holding a sheaf of dried grasses. For today only, find a large poster or photograph of a lion or a group of wild animals. Hang this behind the decoration or to the side or use two such posters as banners behind the altar.

Addition

If you used purple flags in Advent, put them up again, replacing the pink one with a fourth purple one.

Celebration

If possible, arrange to have benediction after Mass today and invite all to stay for this, or have a quiet time after the homily or after communion, and ask that everyone use this time to reflect on their lenten resolutions.

Reflection

The gospel on this first Sunday of Lent tells us that Jesus stayed in the wasteland, the desert, for 40 days and was with the wild beasts. Today's altar decoration reminds that we too are now entering into the desert of Lent, a time that may seem to some of us like a wasteland. In today's difficult world, we too often feel that we are living with the wild beasts—the beasts of career stress and competition, of continual hurry and worry, of sickness and financial problems, of disintegrating family life. We see our children threatened by such "beasts" as drugs, alcoholism, AIDS, a breakdown in our country's educational system and false values. Today, as we begin this penitential season of Lent, take time to step away as Jesus did. Stay after Mass today for Benediction (welcome the quiet time after the homily) and use this time to reflect on your life and what you could do during Lent to start to change it for the better. Do you need to give up something— some temptation or habit that is not healthy for your physical or spiritual life? Or do you need to add something, to resolve to do something new and constructive? Should you come to Mass during the week, say the rosary each day, volunteer to help at a nursing home or at school or at an inner-city soup kitchen or just say one small prayer every day for some special intention? Only you know the beasts of your life. Only you can ask God's help to do battle with them. Ask today.

Second Sunday of Lent

Genesis 22:1-2, 9, 10-13, 15-18
Romans 8, 31:34
Mark 9:2-10

"He was transfigured before their eyes and his clothes be-came dazzling white."

Decoration
Repeat last week's lenten decoration. Or buy one (or two) of those inexpensive long mirrors that are designed to be attached to the back of a bedroom door. Either put one of these horizon-tally in front of the altar and add a bit of greenery on each side or hang two of them vertically where you would usually hang ban-ners behind the altar.

Celebration
Put a large basket in the vestibule and label it with a sign "One a week" or "St.Vincent de Paul Society" or the name of a parish help-group. In today's reflection or homily or in the bulle-tin, ask parishioners to start to bring one can or package of food every week throughout the year to be given to the poor.

Reflection

When Jesus took his friends with him to the mountaintop in today's gospel reading, he was transfigured before their eyes. Our mirror altar decoration suggests that you think today about how you might look if you were transfigured. We of course cannot be transfigured like Jesus but we can be changed and renewed and reformed. One small way to begin is to really think of others, to be aware of their needs, to try to understand how they feel and how they hurt. Each year at Christmas, many people are anxious to share with the less fortunate and they donate baskets of food and gifts. But the poor are not only poor at Christmastime. They get hungry during the rest of the year too. So today, as one small step toward transfiguration, toward becoming aware of the members of our human family who need help all year, we ask that you begin to bring one can or jar or package of non-perishable food every week when you come to Mass. Just one item. One small item would not change your lifestyle nor hurt your budget but it could make a big difference to someone whose family never has enough to eat. We've placed a basket in the vestibule for the one-a-week collection and all food received will be distributed regularly. Add this to your lenten resolutions. Start next week to bring a small food item every week and make a big difference in someone else's life.

THIRD SUNDAY OF LENT

Exodus 20:1-17 or 20, 1-3, 7-8, 12-17
1 Corinthians 1:22-25
John 2:13-25

"Remember to keep holy the Sabbath day..." "He made a (kind of) whip of cords and drove them all out of the temple area...and knocked over the money-changers' tables, spilling their coins."

Decoration

If you have retained the earlier lenten decoration, simply add a whip made of cords. Take some long strips of heavy cord or rope and wrap the top to form a sort of handle. Or use a white linen cloth as a background and sprinkle different kinds and sizes of coins over it, using some foreign coins if you have any. Then add the whip and some greenery.

Addition

Make two banners, each with five of the commandments lettered on them.

Celebration

Ask a neighborhood restaurant or fast-food shop to give you coupons for some kind of discount on a meal today. Or, if your parish sells ads in the bulletin, ask one of the restaurant advertisers to make this week's ad into a discount coupon which parishioners can clip and use only on Sunday.

Reflection

In today's gospel, Jesus uses a whip of cords to drive the money-changers from the Temple. What would Jesus think of today's money-changers who seem dedicated to the idea of business-as-usual seven days a week? One of the commandments repeated in today's first reading reminds us to "keep holy the Sabbath day." Does this mean only to stop for a few minutes to go to Mass and then to resume business as usual? The reading from Exodus goes on to say, "Six days you may labor and do all your work but the seventh day is the sabbath of the Lord, your God. In six days the Lord made the heaven and the earth, the sea and all that is in them; but on the seventh day, he rested. That is why the Lord has blessed the sabbath day and made it holy." Perhaps it's time to meditate on what this reading says to the people of today. Have we become so engrossed in business and money-changing that we have forgotten to take time to rest, to spend time with the family, to enjoy the goodness of the earth God made and gave to us? Take a day off today. Sit quietly and say an extra prayer. Review your lenten resolutions. Think about how you can rearrange your life so that you can take more time off every Sunday to relax and enjoy, to give thanks and praise.

To help you get started on this idea of resting on the sabbath, why not skip the work of cooking a big meal and take the family out to dinner today—or next Sunday! Look in your bulletin today for a coupon (stop at the church door today and pick up a coupon) that will help you relax a bit by enjoying Sunday dinner out with the family. Maybe you might even like to invite an aunt or grandma or lonely neighbor to go along. Resolve today to try to always remember to "keep holy the Sabbath."

FOURTH SUNDAY OF LENT

2 Chronicles 36:14-17, 19-23
Ephesians 2:4-10
John 3:14-21

"The light came into the world, but men loved darkness rather than light.... Everyone who practices evil hates the light; he does not come near it for fear his deeds will be exposed."

Decoration
If you have retained the lenten decoration, you might want to add only some banners with symbols of light. Or you could make the focus of today's decoration a large picture or statue of Jesus and surround it with various types of light: a lantern, a flashlight, candles in different sizes and shapes. Or you could use luminaries—pretty coated paper bags that have cut-out designs. You fill them with sand and then add a vigil light and the light sparkles out through the cut-outs. (You can usually buy these at card shops or any store that features party decorations.)

Celebration
Perhaps you could find someone to donate some book matches—enough to give to each of the adults as they leave Mass today—as a reminder of today's lesson of light. Maybe you could even get someone to pay to have the church's name printed on the matchbooks!

Reflection
Today's gospel tells us that "everyone who practices evil hates the light." Probably most of us—even those who practice small evils—sometimes fear the light, fear having others learn about our failings and failures. But the gospel reassures us that "God did not send the Son into the world to condemn the world but that the world might be saved through him." Jesus, the light of the world, is our beacon, our example, our hope. Today we are distributing matchbooks as a small reminder to abandon the darkness and follow the light. Take this message with you wherever you go this week as a reminder that the one "who acts in the truth comes into the light."

FIFTH SUNDAY OF LENT

Jeremiah 31:31-34
Hebrews 5:7-9
John 12:20-33

"The hour has come.... If anyone would serve me, let him follow me...."

Decoration

Again, if you have retained the lenten decoration, simply add a box wrapped in purple paper. Or make an arrangement of various-sized boxes, each wrapped in various shades of purple paper. Add bows of purple yarn or contrasting shades of purple ribbon or paste on cut-out designs of crosses in white or purple. Add blue vigil lights or a few stalks of purple irises.

Addition

Two banners: one with the design of an hour glass with the sand almost run out; the second with the design of gift boxes.

Celebration

Perhaps have another quiet time today—after the homily or communion—when people can reflect on the success or failure of the lenten resolutions they made earlier.

Reflection

In today's gospel, Jesus says "the hour has come...." We are reminded that time is running out for us too—there are only a few days left in Lent to make good our lenten resolutions. When Lent began, you gave a gift to God, a resolution to make a lenten sacrifice or a promise to serve in some special way. Have you been able to follow through with these resolutions and promises? Spend some quiet time today reflecting on Jesus' words in the gospel: "Unless the grain of wheat falls to the earth and dies, it remains just a grain of wheat....If anyone would serve me, let him follow me...."Jesus asks us each to die to self...to serve in whatever way we are called. Although the days of Lent will soon pass away, it is never too late to reform, to resolve, to serve. Think today what gift you could give in these last days of Lent, perhaps just one prayer every day or one act of kindness or one harsh word left unsaid. The hour has come...how will you serve? What gift will you give?

PASSION SUNDAY
(Palm Sunday)

Isaiah 50:4-7
Philippians 2:6-11
Mark 14:1-15, 47 or 15:1-39

"Are you the king of the Jews?"

Decoration
Today the main decoration will of course be palms. Arrange bouquets of them in tall brass vases. Or make floral arrangements, using palms as background the way you would normally use greenery. Or make bundles of palms and tie them with purple velvet ribbons and place these in front of the main altar and on side altars.

Addition
Letter a sign, KING OF THE JEWS, and attach it to a long pole. Have someone carry this in at the beginning of the entrance procession, followed by children carrying palms, followed by the celebrant.

Celebration
Possibly ask a parishioner to act as Jesus during the reading of the gospel. Choose someone with a beard and perhaps longer hair. Dress him in a long white robe. Bind his hands with ropes and have him led in by two men dressed as soldiers at the point where the gospel says, "They bound Jesus, led him away and handed him over to Pilate." At appropriate times in the reading, have the soldiers put a purple garment on him and then a crown of thorns and then lead him away and off the altar with the words "Led him out to crucify him."

Reflection
Today on Palm Sunday we begin the solemn celebration of Holy Week, recalling the events of the Passover and the Passion of Jesus. According to an ancient custom followed in many countries, the three days following Palm Sunday are spent in house

cleaning: scrubbing, clearing out, throwing away, preparing the home for spring and Easter. This custom probably began as a continuation of the ancient Jewish practice of cleaning to prepare for the Passover. Today, as we hear the gospel about Passover activities and enter into Holy Week, perhaps you would like to consider following this spring cleaning custom in your home. It's a project parents and children can work on together and plan to complete before the Easter triduum begins on Holy Thursday. Turn off the television, forget cooking and have sandwich meals and work together to bring new life into your home. And, as you go through closets, the garage, the basement, save any usable clothing or household goods and donate these to our parish St. Vincent de Paul Society to be distributed to the poor. This will be a Holy Week activity that can benefit you and the children and the people who receive your donations.

Mass of the Lord's Supper
The only decoration you will need this evening are supplies for the washing of the feet. But, since this evening recalls the

breaking of the bread, perhaps you might put an announcement in an earlier bulletin and ask parishioners to bring gifts of bread and bakery goods this evening. Decorate a side altar with white flowers and a few loaves of pretty, unsliced bread and some vigil lights. Have a special table set up near this—or in the vestibule— where people can place their gifts. Announce that these bakery items will be given to one of the local kitchens that serve the poor so they can be used for breakfast on Easter Sunday morning. (Call one of these places ahead of time and arrange to have the bakery goods delivered so they can be frozen or used while still fresh.)

Good Friday

In addition to the usual Good Friday liturgy, you may wish to follow the custom of the flower cross. Ask each parishioner to bring along one real or artificial flower this day. Or have a large basket of flowers at the door and ask each person to take one of these flowers as they enter. After the veneration of the cross, bring out a large wooden cross and place it on the floor in front of the altar. Ask everyone to come forward and place their flower on the cross. As the people watch, the stark bare cross will turn into a glorious cross in bloom with beauty.

Easter Vigil

Decorations for the Easter vigil will be the same as those for Easter Sunday. You might wish to keep some of the bakery items brought on Holy Thursday and invite parishioners to share these with coffee or hot chocolate for an Easter vigil celebration after Mass. Or you might like to have large Easter baskets filled with candy Easter eggs or other wrapped candy and invite each one present to break their fast and begin the Easter celebration by helping themselves to a treat as they leave church.

EASTER SUNDAY

Acts 10:34, 37-43
Colossians 3:1-4
John 20:1-9

"Since you have been raised up in company with Christ, set your heart on what pertains to higher realms.... Be intent on things above rather than on things on earth...."

Decoration

Be intent on things above! Fly high today! Find as many pretty kites as you can and hang them by threads from the ceiling of the church behind the altar and maybe even all along the side aisles! What could better illustrate the message "He is risen"? In addition, you could put a pretty arrangement in front of the altar of all white flowers or an assortment of bright spring blossoms.

Celebration

Since most people will be going home for family celebrations today, you only need to remind them to start their Easter meal with a family prayer. Put a note in the bulletin suggesting the start of a new family tradition, a holiday litany. At the start of the meal, the father or mother could begin and then others follow by saying, "This Easter is an alleluia for me because _____ ." As each person names a personal reason for rejoicing, the rest respond with "For this alleluia, we thank you, Lord." If your parish has a large number of parishioners who might not have a celebration to attend, you could have a small Easter gathering after one of the Masses with coffee, sweet rolls, and boiled and decorated Easter eggs.

Reflection

Today's decorations remind us to look up, to let our thoughts turn heavenward on this holy day when all the earth rejoices in the amazing news, "He is Risen!" In the second reading we are also told to "get rid of the old yeast and make of yourselves fresh dough, unleavened loaves." This refers to the Jewish custom of making bread each day by taking a piece of leftover dough which had been allowed to decay and mixing it into the fresh dough to act as the yeast, the leaven. At Passover, they threw out the old dough and ate unleavened bread, symbolically throwing out the decay and celebrating Passover with a clean heart. Jesus is our new, unleavened bread, free of decay, the Savior who has fulfilled the old Law by bringing the new. During Lent, we too have cast out the decay of old habits and now we can let our alleluias soar heavenward, rejoicing as we celebrate the resurrection with our own newness, our own resurrection to new life and a new beginning.

SECOND SUNDAY OF EASTER

Acts 4:32-35
1 John 5:1-6
John 20:19-31

"I'll never believe it without probing the nail-prints in his hands, without putting my finger in the nail-marks and my hand into his side."

Decoration

You will want to leave the Easter decorations from last Sunday so the only thing you will need today is some decorated baskets for the celebration. Or you might want to make some wind chimes from nails and hang them in the vestibule where the air will hit them as people come and go.

Celebration

Today ask some of the liturgy committee or greeters to stand at the door with baskets filled with large nails from the hardware store. Distribute these to parishioners as they are leaving. Or leave the baskets of nails in a prominent place so people can help themselves.

Reflection

In today's gospel, doubting Thomas does not believe that his friends have seen the risen Lord and protests that he will not believe until he can see and feel the nail-marks left from the crucifixion. How many times have you challenged the Lord in this way, demanding proof of his presence? How many times have you questioned God's work in your life and demanded proof of his existence, his presence, his love? When the other disciples rejoiced in the Lord's presence, he said to them, "Peace be with you." When he proved himself to Thomas, he said, "Blessed are they who have not seen and have believed." Today, at each church door, there will be baskets filled with nails. Take one home with you and look at it every day this week. Ask yourself if you are like Thomas, always demanding to see the nail marks, demanding proof. In today's world, there is so little trust: between husband and wife, employer and employee, children and teachers. And sometimes the lack of trust in other humans is justified. But no matter how many times you are betrayed by the world, you can trust in the Lord. Look at the nail, surrender, believe, accept. Put your complete trust in the Lord and rejoice in his peace.

THIRD SUNDAY OF EASTER

Acts 3:13-15, 17-19
1 John 2:1-5
Luke 24:35-48

"They gave him a piece of cooked fish, which he took and ate in their presence....He opened their minds to the understanding of the Scriptures."

Decoration
If the Easter decorations are not still in place, you could make an arrangement today using a large serving dish shaped like a fish—or any kind of large ceramic or glass fish—and add a picture of the risen Jesus, a candle, ferns or other greenery. If you cannot find an appropriate fish symbol, make an arrangement of various covered casseroles interspersed with greenery.

Celebration
In today's gospel, Jesus ate with his friends and then "opened their minds to the understanding of the Scriptures." So this

might be a nice after-Easter time to plan a parish potluck supper for Sunday afternoon or evening, and invite a guest speaker to talk about Scripture! Someone will have to publicize it and make arrangements to set up tables, and so forth, in advance. Greeters could be stationed at the door and greet each person with "Peace to you" as Jesus said to his friends in today's gospel, or you could ask each person to turn to someone close by and extend this greeting at the beginning of the meal.

Reflection

Whenever something extraordinary happens, friends just can't wait to get together and talk about it to each other and discuss all the details—so it's easy to imagine the scene in today's gospel where the disciples are all talking about Jesus on the road to Emmaus. But then, when he appears suddenly in their midst, even the disciples, his closest friends, are startled and frightened. This too is easy to imagine since we are all sometimes frightened by surprises—especially by the kind of surprises that God often presents us. Jesus knew just how to calm his friends, though—he ate with them. Have you noticed that we too celebrate both happy and sad occasions—baptisms, birthdays, weddings, funerals or just weekends—by having something to eat with friends! After Jesus ate the fish, he spoke to the gathering and "opened their minds to the understanding of the Scriptures." This week, we are combining both of these ideas from today's gospel by sharing a potluck supper and having an after-dinner speaker who will "open our minds" with a talk about Scripture! All are invited.

FOURTH SUNDAY OF EASTER

Acts 4:8-12
1 John 3:1-2
John 10:11-18

*"This Jesus is 'the stone rejected by you the builders which
has become the cornerstone.'"*

Decoration

Take a photograph of the cornerstone of your church and then
have the photograph enlarged as large as possible. Paste this on
stiff cardboard and place it in front of the altar today, flanked by
arrangements of flowers or greenery. Or if you can't get a photograph, simply use a large stone to represent a cornerstone.

Addition

Make two banners: one covered with little wooly sheep and
the other with the design of a shepherd's crook.

Celebration

Ask the school children or some committee to cut out paper
figures of a stick person, using white paper or various colors of
construction paper. Pass these out as people come in the door or
some time during the Mass. Provide pencils in the pews so people can write on these figures and either have someone collect
the figures or have baskets at the church door where people can
deposit these before they leave.

Reflection

Our decoration today is a photo of the cornerstone of our own
church, a stone which was laid ____(date)____. This is a reminder
of the first reading where we hear that Jesus is the cornerstone...a
reminder of the second reading where we are told of the love the
Father has bestowed on us by letting us be called children of
God...a reminder of the gospel story of the good shepherd who
lays down his life for the sheep in his flock. Jesus is our cornerstone and each new church built extends his ministry and each
person in that church continues his work on earth. Today, as you
meditate on the readings, think of some person you know who

54

has followed Jesus' example and been a cornerstone in your life, someone who has supported you and helped you build a better life, someone who has also been a protector, a shepherd to watch over you.

We have passed out (you will find in the pews) some "paper people." Please take one of those and write on it the name of the person who has been your personal cornerstone. Drop that in the basket at the back of church as you leave today so that we can honor these people by adding them to a banner for next Sunday's liturgy. And during the week, take a few moments to say a little prayer of thanksgiving for that special person in your life, along with a prayer of thanksgiving for Jesus, the shepherd who saved us all.

FIFTH SUNDAY OF EASTER

Acts 9:26-31
1 John 3:18-24
John 15:1-8

"I am the true vine and my Father is the vinegrower. He trims away every barren branch but the fruitful ones he trims clean to increase their yield."

Decoration

Today find a flowering tree or bush and cut some branches. Put a large arrangement in front of the altar. Or put the flowering arrangements in low vases on side altars or in tall vases at each side of the main altar. Then, in front of the altar, put an arrangement of dead branches or vines along with some pruning shears and gardener's gloves.

Addition

Hang banners which you have made by pasting the cutout figures from last week's liturgy onto large pieces of felt or cardboard. There will probably be too many to use them all for altar banners so you could make a large banner for the vestibule and add all the leftover names. Be sure to use as many as possible because people will probably look through them, trying to find the one they made last week. (If you have white paper people, put them on a colored background; if you have used multi-color construction paper for the people, paste them on a white or pastel background for contrast.)

Celebration

In many areas of the country, organizations and church groups are participating in a program called Adopt-a-Highway. People call the highway department and are assigned a certain section of a local highway, usually somewhere near their neighborhoods. Then they take trash bags and go along the highway picking up litter. They promise to do this on a regular basis so this keeps the area neat and also frees highway workers to do other types of roadwork. If you have that program in your area,

56

you might get together a parish group to sign up for this program or you could start your own litter collection! If your churchyard or athletic field or some neighborhood park or public area nearby needs a facelift, get together a group that will report regularly to pick up, clean up, fix-up, and de-litter. Announce this program in the bulletin today.

Reflection

Today's decoration reflects the gospel in which Jesus says he is the vine and we are the branches. Jesus also points out that the Father, the vinegrower, prunes away barren branches and trims clean the fruitful ones so they can be even more productive. We are reminded that sometimes the trimming in our lives hurts—but then helps. The banners today display the names of the people you gave us last week, people who were fruitful branches, people who helped you and shepherded you and maybe even did some of the trimming to make your life bear good fruit. Since others have helped you, perhaps it is now your turn to help others. There are many parish groups that would be so happy to welcome you and we are introducing still another one today: the Adopt-a-Highway program. Check the bulletin for details about this pick-up, fix-up, clean-up idea. Join this group or some other parish organization so that you can help others and yourself become a more fruitful branch.

SIXTH SUNDAY OF EASTER

Acts 10:25-26, 34-35
1 John 4:7-10
John 15:9-17

"The command I give you is this: that you love one another."

Decoration

Today use a selection of colorful greeting cards, including some religious ones. Put some in a pretty basket tied with ribbons. Stand up some so the designs will show. Add a second basket with some envelopes in it that have already been addressed. In front, put an addressed envelope and some ballpoint pens. On each side, include a small flowering plant, the kind you might take as a gift to someone in the hospital.

Addition

You might like to use banners with some kind of design that indicates love or one that depicts commandments and a second that depicts love.

Celebration

Many parishes include in the Sunday bulletin each week the names of parishioners who have been hospitalized and the name of the hospital where each is recuperating. If your parish does not do this, today would be a good time to start. If it does, call attention to this fact today and encourage other parishioners to include those who are ill in their prayers and to let them know they are missed and remembered by sending them get-well cards. You might also include in the bulletin today the names and addresses of nursing homes in your area along with a message encouraging parishioners to volunteer their services there or to adopt one particular resident who seldom has visitors and send cards and possibly small gifts to that person on a regular basis. You might also suggest that parishioners donate used magazines and books to the area nursing homes.

Reflection

In today's readings, the word "love" is mentioned nineteen times. The message for today is obvious: love God, love others. Some members of God's family who need a great deal of love and attention—but are often overlooked—are those who are in hospitals and nursing homes. In today's bulletin, and in every week's bulletin, we list the names of parishioners who have been hospitalized. Today we are also listing names and addresses of area nursing homes. Our altar decoration is a reminder that one way to show love to others is by sending cheery greeting cards to those who are sick and by taking time to call or drop by or send a little gift or flowering plant to those in nursing homes. This is such a small thing to do; it doesn't take much time or money, but it can make a big difference to someone who is feeling forgotten. This week, think especially about the last words of today's gospel and consider what you could do to follow this direction: "The command I give you is this: that you love one another."

SEVENTH SUNDAY OF EASTER

Acts 1:15-17, 20-26
1 John 4:11-16
John 17:11-19

"I gave them your word.... Consecrate them by means of truth. 'Your word is the truth.'"

Decoration

The focus of today's decoration will certainly be easy to obtain, a Bible. Put an open Bible in the center of your decoration, surrounded by flowers or greenery. The week before, ask someone to type up several sheets of popular biblical passages and then photocopy them and cut them into strips so there will be enough strips for each parishioner to take home one biblical quote. Put these into baskets and place them at the outer edges of the decoration.

Celebration

At the end of Mass, have children come up to the altar and take the baskets and process out before the celebrant and stand at each church door. As parishioners are leaving, each person can reach into the basket and choose his or her own message.

Reflection

In today's gospel, Jesus tells the Father, "I gave them your word." He says it is time for him to return to the Father and prays for the Father to protect and guard us, his people. He says that as the Father sent him, he now sends us. Today's decoration reminds us that Jesus has given us the Father's word, which is the truth. But do we really appreciate the word and study it and live by it? The baskets in our decoration contain short Scripture passages: the word, the truth. At the end of Mass today, these will be taken to the church doors. As you are leaving, we invite you each to reach into the basket and choose one of the slips of paper. During the week, read it over and over. It is a message to you from Jesus...from the Father. It is the word. Think about that message...meditate on it...ponder it. Perhaps it is a message that could change your life.

PENTECOST SUNDAY

Acts 2:1-11
1 Corinthians 12:3-7, 12-13
John 20:19-23

"Tongues of fire appeared which parted and came to rest on each of them. All were filled with the Holy Spirit. They began to express themselves in foreign tongues... there were devout Jews of every nation under heaven... each one heard these men speaking his own language."

Decoration

Simply use one large banner today behind the altar with the design of tongues of fire. You could make the bottom part of the design a semi-circle of a fabric in a busy design—possibly a multi-colored flower design—to suggest the idea of many different kinds of people. Have large, brilliant tongues of fire descending and use a bright, aqua background behind the red to make it really stand out starkly. You might add a large border of macramé and heavy fringe both at the top and bottom to make the banner very impressive and eye-catching.

Celebration

If your parish includes people of various ethnic backgrounds, or if there is a college nearby where you might find students who speak various languages, ask several people to do the first reading today with each person reading just a few lines in his or her native language. The first few lines could be read in Spanish and then the next person could read the next few lines in French and then another read a few lines in German....At the end, the lector could read the entire reading in English. Or you could have a multi-national tasting meal this weekend with a mixture of foods from different countries: Italian spaghetti, Chinese stir-fry, Russian borscht, or whatever someone in your parish knows how to prepare. You could charge for this meal and give the proceeds to Pro-Life or some other parish group.

Reflection

Today we joyfully celebrate Pentecost Sunday, the birthday of our church. In the first reading, we hear how tongues of fire appeared and came to rest on the brethren and all were filled with the Holy Spirit. Our reading today in different languages reflects the idea that on that first Pentecost, the apostles spoke in foreign tongues and people of all different nations could understand them. It is also a reminder that often, even when the readings are in our own tongue, sometimes we fail to listen closely enough to understand them—and to benefit from the message. To continue this idea of the gift of tongues and understanding, we invite you to a multi-national tasting party. We will have food (and entertainment) representing many tongues and many nations. See the bulletin for details.

TRINITY SUNDAY

Deuteronomy 4:32-34, 39-40
Romans 8:14-17
Matthew 28:16-20

"Go, therefore, and make disciples of all the nations. Baptize them in the name of the Father and of the Son, and of the Holy Spirit."

Decoration

Go to a religious goods store and buy (or borrow) several pretty holy water fonts, the kind you would display in your home. Or you may be able to borrow some from friends. There are many different beautiful designs available today. Arrange some greenery as a background to show off the designs.

Addition

Banners depicting baptism: a baptismal font, hands pouring water from a shell or other container, a priest's hands raised in blessing, etc.

Celebration

At one time, the once-popular custom of having a holy water font in the home waned but recently it seems to be returning. This would be a good time to purchase a variety of fonts and offer them for sale in the vestibule—suggesting them as gifts for newlyweds, new parents, children.... You might also have some containers of holy water available for parishioners to take home. (Many parishes save baby food jars and put holy water in these and have them available at a certain place in the vestibule so that parishioners can always find holy water to refill their fonts.)

Reflection

For many years, it was the custom for most Catholic homes to have a holy water font. Sometimes it hung by the door so that you could take a bit of holy water and bless yourself as you came in or went out. Sometimes it hung in the children's room so they could bless themselves before they went to bed at night. Today many families are rediscovering this old and beautiful custom and have chosen holy water fonts similar to those in our altar decoration today. Having holy water in your home and as part of your daily life is a constant reminder of your own baptism, of your membership in the family of God. It is also a reminder of today's gospel when Jesus tells his disciples to go out and make disciples of others so that they too may be baptized "in the name of the Father and of the Son and of the Holy Spirit." The holy water is a reminder that you are Jesus' disciples today. For those who would like to have a holy water font in their home, or would like to give one as a gift to newlyweds or to new parents, we are having a sale in the vestibule today of a variety of fonts. Today and every Sunday there will also be containers of holy water in the vestibule for you to take home. (You might mention where these will be kept in the vestibule—or in the rectory.)

THE BODY AND BLOOD OF CHRIST
(Corpus Christi)

Exodus 24:3-8
Hebrews 9:11-15
Mark 14, 12-16:22-26

"During the meal, he took bread, blessed and broke it, and gave it to them. 'Take this,' he said; 'this is my body.' He likewise took a cup, gave thanks and passed it to them, and they all drank from it. He said to them, 'This is my blood.'"

Decoration

Today's best decoration would be the obvious: stalks of wheat and bunches of grapes and perhaps a loaf of bread and a goblet or chalice of wine. You could arrange the wheat in a tall brass container or tie it into a bundle. You could have the grapes overflowing a basket or arranged in a pretty bowl. Perhaps rather than hanging a banner in a separate place, you could incorporate it into the arrangement. On the banner, use a figure in a robe with arms outstretched but use the design of a host and chalice to form the head and neck, graphically illustrating the idea of body and blood, host and chalice.

Celebration

Again, an obvious but appropriate celebration for today would be a parish communion breakfast—either in the church hall or at a nearby restaurant. You might use this occasion to honor new parishioners who have registered in the parish within recent months. Or you could ask some children to wear their First Holy Communion clothes today and bring up the offertory gifts.

Reflection

What is the most important moment of your week, of your day? No matter what else happens to you each week, the most important moment is when you receive the body and blood of Christ in the eucharist. Today's decoration reflects the gospel reading that tells us Jesus actually gave us his own body and his own blood—a share of his life. What could be more important than that? On this special feast day, think about how lucky we are in America to be able to not only worship freely on Sundays but also to have Mass every single day in most Catholic churches across the land. Do you take advantage of this special blessing? Do you attend daily Mass whenever possible? Perhaps this is the day you could promise yourself to start participating in the eucharistic celebration during the week as well as on Sundays. What better gift could you give yourself? We invite you to join us today for a communion breakfast, honoring the newest parishioners of our parish.

Sixth Sunday in Ordinary Time

Leviticus 13:1-2, 44-46
1 Corinthians 10:31-11
1 Mark 1:40-45

"The man went off and began to proclaim the whole matter freely, making the story public."

Decoration
Ring the bell today! Try to find several pretty or interesting bells of all different sizes and varieties. You might cover some boxes with fabric and use these as stands to display the bells at different heights so they would show up better. And, as usual, add a bit of greenery.

Celebration
Does your parish proclaim the news freely? If not, maybe it's time to start a parish newsletter! What better way to promote a spirit of community than to keep the community informed of what's going on! The announcements in the bulletin give the bare bones of what's happening in the parish but a newsletter could include much more: bits and pieces of news and views, stories of church developments around the country or around the world, and maybe a few laughs too. Announce this possibility in the bulletin today and advertise for some newshounds who might be willing to take on such a project.

Reflection
Can you imagine what it must have been like to be a leper: shunned by all, sometimes forced to ring a bell to announce your presence in a crowd and call "unclean" so others could move aside and be careful to not even touch you or get close to you? How lonely and frightening that must have been. But the leper in today's gospel still had the courage and the faith to approach Jesus and ask to be cured. When Jesus took pity on him, no wonder the man proclaimed the news of his miraculous cure to all who would listen. Our altar decoration reminds us that we too should ring out the good news, tell of the wonders of our faith and proclaim our salvation.

SEVENTH SUNDAY IN ORDINARY TIME

Isaiah 43:18-19, 21-22, 24-25
2 Corinthians 1:18-22
Mark 2:1-12

*"...they let down the mat on which the paralytic was lying....
Jesus said, 'Stand up, pick up your mat and walk again.'"*

Decoration
Place a large straw mat in front of the altar and simply lay a pair of crutches on it. Or if your church has steps going up to the altar, lay the mat and crutches on these so they will be more visible.

Celebration
If you have the Special Olympics program in your area, you might invite a speaker to come today to explain the program and enlist volunteers. Or if you have a special religion program for handicapped students, you could invite someone to speak about that. Or you could simply list in the bulletin the various ways in which parishioners could volunteer to help the disabled in your parish or your town.

Reflection
The paralyzed man in today's gospel must have had really great friends! They just wouldn't give up. Even if it meant "raising the roof," they were determined to get their friend near enough to Jesus to get help for him. We would all be fortunate to have such good friends. We are all paralyzed or disabled in some way, perhaps not physically but in other ways. We are paralyzed by fear or laziness or hopelessness or sin. Look around you to help others but look also at yourself. What kind of paralysis is keeping you from getting closer to Jesus?

EIGHTH SUNDAY IN ORDINARY TIME

Hosea 2:16-17, 21-22
2 Corinthians 3:1-6
Mark 2:18-22

"I will espouse you to me forever.... I will espouse you in fidelity, and you shall know the Lord."

Decoration
Focus today's decoration on a wedding motif. Center it with something indicative of a wedding: the top from a wedding cake, a music box with a bride and groom on top or even a wedding photo. Surround this with poufs or bows of white net, strings of pearls or crystal beads, white candles....

Celebration
Make photo copies of this ancient Hebrew prayer and pass it out at the door or in the pews, or reprint it in the bulletin:

From childhood to maturity
   and youth to age;
From innocence to awareness
   and ignorance to knowing;
From foolishness to discretion and then,
   perhaps, to wisdom;
From weakness to strength
   or strength to weakness—and, often, back again;
From health to sickness and back, we pray,
   to health again;
From offense to forgiveness,
From loneliness to love,
From joy to gratitude,
From pain to compassion,
And grief to understanding—from fear to faith;
From defeat to defeat to defeat....

Until, looking backward or ahead,
   We see that victory lies
   Not at some high place along the way,
But in having made the Journey, stage by stage.

Reflection

The altar decoration reflects words from each of the three readings today. In the first, we hear, "I will espouse you to me forever...and you shall know the Lord." And then we go to the second reading to hear, "You are my letter, known and read to all men, written on your hearts." And finally, the gospel speaks of the bridegroom and of pouring new wine into new skins. We have been espoused to the Lord forever. People should be able to look at us and read his message. We must make ourselves into new skins so that we can be filled with new life. Please take home a copy of the prayer we are distributing today and meditate on the words...from childhood to maturity, from innocence to awareness, from defeat to defeat, the victory lies in having made the Journey, stage by stage.

Ninth Sunday in Ordinary Time

Deuteronomy 5:12-15
2 Corinthians 4:6-11
Mark 2:23-3, 6 or 2, 23-28

"The sabbath was made for man, not man for the sabbath."

Decoration
Make a large calendar today of posterboard—not for the entire month but just for one week. List various activities on each day: Monday, get to work early, Scout meeting at 7; Tuesday, make cupcakes for class party, attend political rally; Wednesday, dentist appointment; Thursday, grocery shop, dinner meeting.... List whatever type of activities might be appropriate for your parishioners. Then, on Sunday, print in large letters: REST. Put a stack of small rocks at each end of the calendar or put the rocks into two baskets.

Celebration
Invite people to stay after Mass or return to the church later in the afternoon and take one of the rocks in the decoration and place it on a side altar and light a candle, symbolically taking their burdens and giving them to God.

Reflection
Today's readings remind us once again to rest on the sabbath, to keep this day holy and use it for the Lord. For many years, this day was set aside for fun and family togetherness but in today's busy world, the sabbath is sometimes even more hurried and stressful than other days of the week. So many seem burdened down with work and worry. In our decoration today, we have placed some small rocks to symbolize the weight of life's cares. Take a few minutes after Mass today or come back to church later this afternoon and go the altar and take one of the rocks. Think about it as a burden in your life. Take the rock and place it on the left side altar and light a candle. Tell God that you are giving your burden to him because it is too heavy for you to carry alone and you need some rest. Offer up your problems and worries to the Lord today and be at peace. Rest.

TENTH SUNDAY IN ORDINARY TIME

Genesis 3:9-15
2 Corinthians 4:13–5:1
1 Mark 3:20-35

"You have eaten, then, from the tree of which I had forbidden you to eat!"

Decoration
Today simply make an arrangement of large, beautiful, red apples. Arrange them in baskets or bowls or stack them into a pyramid, using greenery here and there as a contrast. Hollow out a small section in the top of other apples, just large enough to make them into candleholders. Add tall white candles and a sprig of greenery to each of these and use them to flank the center arrangement. Or make a long spray of greenery and add apples all along it, interspersed with red vigil lights.

Celebration
Ask the school children or a committee to make up cards with the drawing of an apple and the word WHY? Give these out to all parishioners today.

Reflection
"You have eaten from the tree of which I had forbidden you to eat. Why? Why?" In today's first reading, God confronts Adam and Eve and asks them why they have done what was forbidden. And they are ashamed. But in the second reading we hear the reassuring words, "Do not lose heart because our inner being is renewed each day." And then the gospel reminds us that sins will be forgiven. Perhaps one of the greatest sins of today's society is the immorality presented on television and in videos— immorality presented as the normal way to live, the accepted way, the correct way. We know this is not God's way but we say nothing and do nothing to keep our children from being constantly besieged by these false values. Today we are passing out a small card that we would like you to take home and tape to the top of your television screen. Attach it so that it will be easy to

see and will serve as a reminder every day. It has a simple design: an apple to remind you of that first sin and the word "Why?" to remind you of God's question. Perhaps this card will help you to remember to take action. When you see a program that presents immorality of any kind as a proper and accepted way of life, turn off that program. If you have children, explain to them why that is not an appropriate program to watch. Don't give in. Remember, the first time you see something that goes against your Christian principles, you are shocked! The second time you see it, you are just surprised and perhaps uncomfortable. The next time—you've seen it before and it doesn't seem too bad. And finally, when you see it, you accept it as just the way things are. You quickly forget that it is not God's way, not the Christian way, not the truth. That's what is happening to our children today—and also to adults who should know better. Police yourself and your family. Let the little apple card remind you to turn off programs that do not belong in your home. Call or write television stations and tell them you have stopped watching their shows. Write to sponsors and tell them which shows you think they should not sponsor. Just a few television executives have used their power to bring trash into our homes. It's time for us to use our Christian power to get rid of it.

ELEVENTH SUNDAY IN ORDINARY TIME

Ezekiel 17:22-24
2 Corinthians 5:6-10
Mark 4:26-34

"It is like the mustard seed which, when planted in the soil,
is the smallest of all the earth's seeds, yet once it is sown,
springs up to become the largest of shrubs, with branches big
enough for the birds of the sky to build nests in its shade."

Decoration
Time to chop down a tree! Or trim a bush. Or at least find
some branches with lots of pretty green leaves. Add a small flock
of artificial birds tucked here and there in the foliage and perhaps even a bird nest with some bright marbles in it to look like
eggs, or maybe some tiny leftover Easter eggs.

Celebration
Perhaps today you could give out packets of mustard seeds.
Either buy some from a garden supply store (ask for a discount
on a large order!) or buy some loose seed and package it in small
plastic zip-top bags.

Reflection
The familiar story of the mustard seed, the tiny seed that
grows into a bush large enough for birds to nest in its branches,
is told in today's gospel. Sometimes we all feel tiny and insignificant. But even the mustard seed was not insignificant to God—
and neither are we. To God, there is no insignificant person. And
no insignificant work. Whatever you do, if you do it well, it is
pleasing to God. We have often heard that our faith must grow
like the mustard seed but what do we do about it? Do we cultivate our faith? Even the mustard seed needs nourishment and
care in order to flourish. To make a small start today, stop by the
vestibule and pick up a pamphlet from the rack. Or to make a
bigger leap, join a Catholic study club, start to read religious
books, or set aside just a few minutes each day to read the Bible
or to pray for guidance. Cultivate your faith and as it grows, enjoy the comfort of its shade.

TWELFTH SUNDAY IN ORDINARY TIME

Job 38:1, 8-11
2 Corinthians 5:14-17
Mark 4:35-41

"The waves were breaking over the boat and it began to ship water badly. Jesus was...sound asleep....he awoke and rebuked the wind...and everything grew calm."

Decoration
Make a colorful decoration today using bright plastic rainhats (those big yellow ones that you see in pictures of commercial fishermen on a boat in a stormy sea) and maybe even a slicker or other raingear like hip boots that might be worn in a storm at sea today.

Addition
Banners with the design of stormy waves.

Celebration
Put a notice in the bulletin today with a message similar to this: "Each day this week, at the end of the day, gather the family together (or sit quietly by yourself for a few minutes) and think of the best thing that happened to you that day. It's so easy to recall the bad things that happen to us. This week, think of the good things—and share them. Tell the rest of the family or a friend or neighbor. After a week, it just might become a habit! You might begin to notice the good that comes into your life every day and recall the words from today's gospel, 'Why are you so terrified? Why are you so lacking in faith?'"

Reflection
"Why are you so terrified? Why are you lacking in faith?" These words in today's gospel hit home with all of us at one time or another, or maybe even all the time. Are you terrified? Do you see only bad things happening around you? Our decorations today suggest stormy weather, the kind of squall that blew up when Jesus and his friends were in the boat, the kind of trou-

bling time that comes to all lives. The disciples finally went to Jesus for help, just as we too can go to Jesus. In the bulletin today, we suggest that every day for a week, you try a simple idea. At the end of each day, either alone or with your family, sit down and think about the best thing that happened to you that day. If you're with the family, take turns telling each other about the happening. It's so easy to recall something bad that happens—a traffic jam, a problem with schoolwork, an accident, or just a long wait in the supermarket line—but what about all the little nice things? Think about this at the end of each day for a week, and after that it just might become a good habit! It might even become a family tradition—to share good things each day. It might even make you remember to take your problems to Jesus and to recall the words of today's gospel: "Why are you so terrified? Why are you lacking in faith?"

THIRTEENTH SUNDAY IN ORDINARY TIME

Wisdom 1:13-15; 2:23-24
2 Corinthians 8:7–9, 13-15
Mark 5:21-43 or 5:21-24, 35-43

"Just as you are rich in every respect...you may also abound in your work of charity....The relief of others ought not to impoverish you; there should be a certain equality....A man named Jairus made this earnest appeal: 'My little daughter is critically ill. Please come and lay your hands on her so that she may get well and live.'"

Decoration
Today make a decoration using some expensive or exotic flowers, possibly the bird of paradise flower. Or make a flower arrangement using a very showy silver container with silver candelabra...to look very elegant.

Addition
Make two banners to illustrate rich and poor. On one banner depict lots of money—stacks of bills with piles of coins or opened money bags with gold coins pouring forth. On the other, show a threadbare coin purse opened with just a few coins spilling out.

Celebration

We frequently ask everyone to bring gifts for the poor or to offer prayers for them—but what about the rich? Today, ask everyone to pray for the members of God's family who are wealthy! Include a brief message about this in today's bulletin.

Reflection

Today's elegant altar decoration makes us think of those who are well-to-do, rich enough to live well, to indulge in luxuries, to travel to exotic lands (perhaps we might even think of them as birds of paradise). It's very easy to be jealous of those who have more than we do, just as it is easy to pity those who have less. We frequently offer prayers and donations for those who are less fortunate than we are but how often do we offer concern and prayers for the members of God's family who have more than we do? Fame and fortune do not guarantee happiness. Wealth is no bar against troubles. The rich as well as the poor know about disappointments, sickness, loneliness. In today's gospel, Jairus is described as an official of the synagogue, a leader. He was probably not a poor man but he was a man of faith. And Jesus answered his plea for help and went with him to cure his daughter. The second reading today reminds us to "abound in your work of charity" but it also points out that "the relief of others should not impoverish you; there should be a certain equality." This week, do something different! Say a prayer each day for the wealthy, the powerful, the important. Remember that God made the simple daisy and dandelion but he also made elegant flowers like those in today's decoration. There is room for both in God's garden. Let there be room for both in our hearts and prayers.

Fourteenth Sunday in Ordinary Time

Ezekiel 2:2-5
2 Corinthians 12:7-10
Mark 6:1-6

"How is it such miraculous deeds are accomplished by his hands? Isn't this the carpenter, the son of Mary...'no prophet is without honor except in his native place, among his own kindred, and in his own house.'"

Decoration

Make a display of greenery or flowers and center it with a beautiful picture of Jesus. Then add a placard or a ribbon streamer with these words lettered on it: MAN OF THE YEAR.

Celebration

Have a parish testimonial dinner. Invite all parishioners to come to honor the parish leaders: priests, deacons, presidents of organizations, school board members, school principal.... Have a picture of Jesus with flowers and candles on each table. Ask someone to serve as a toastmaster or toastmistress who will make a short talk about Jesus being our leader, our Man of every Year but then follow this with a few words about parish leaders and their valuable service. Perhaps each could be asked to stand. But then point out that there are many other parishioners who also serve. Perhaps you could invite them to stand: room mothers, people who visit nursing homes, those who wash altar linens or decorate the altar.... If this would be too time consuming, point out that all parishioners are important to the parish and ask all who have not been introduced to stand and have the honorees give them a hand!

Reflection

"Isn't this the carpenter, the son of Mary? How is it such miraculous deeds are accomplished by his hands?" When Jesus went to his own part of the country in today's gospel, the people were amazed. They couldn't believe one of their own could be someone so special. Jesus was too much for them! And Jesus responded by saying that a prophet is only without honor in his own neighborhood, in his own house. That is still true today. We often overlook the work and accomplishments of our own family, our own brothers and sisters in God's family. This week, honor your own. Notice all the good things they do, all that they accomplish in their lives. And then tell them. Let them know how much you appreciate them. And do the same with Jesus. Our altar decoration shows that he is our *Man of the Year*, this year and every year. Don't just pray to ask for something. Remember always to also offer prayers of praise and thanksgiving. In keeping with this gospel, we have planned a parish testimonial dinner to recognize and to honor all those who contribute so much by their work in our own parish. Please join us. Dinner information is in the bulletin.

Fifteenth Sunday in Ordinary Time

Amos 7:12-15
Ephesians 1:3-14 or 1, 3-10
Mark 6:7-13

"He instructed them to take nothing on the journey but a walking stick—no food, no traveling bag, not a coin in the purses in their belts. They were, however, to wear sandals."

Decoration

What better decoration today than a walking stick! Find a craggy, rugged looking one, or just a sturdy stick or tree branch that might look like a crude walking stick. Add a pair of old sandals and the usual greenery. You might use burlap for the background and maybe add a few rough rocks to indicate the roadside.

Celebration

Many parishes around the country participate in programs to help today's homeless. If you have such a program, you could outline this in the bulletin today and ask for helpers. If you don't, perhaps you could get together a small committee to start such a program. In some cities, four or five parishes band together to plan a meal and overnight accomodations for the homeless once a week. With at least four parishes participating, each parish's turn comes only once a month. Those who work with the homeless spread the word about where they should meet to be picked up. Someone volunteers to drive a van and pick up a group of homeless people each Sunday night. They are brought to the auditorium or cafeteria of one of the participating parishes where parishioners have prepared a hot meal and have brought in a portable television so that their guests can watch television after dinner. Then they bring out blankets and pillows and possibly simple foam mattresses to be used for sleeping that night. Two or more parish men volunteer to spend the night there to handle any problems. In the morning, some of the women return to provide a simple breakfast of hot rolls and coffee or bring in breakfasts purchased at a fast-food restaurant. The van then returns the homeless to the place where they were picked up. The next week, a different parish provides the hospitality. It isn't much but at least the homeless have somewhere to eat and sleep once a week.

Reflection

One of the tragedies of our country today is the fact that we have many homeless people who are out on our streets with little more than the walking stick mentioned in today's gospel. Jesus tells his disciples to leave on a journey without any food or traveling bag or even a coin. Many of America's homeless travel this same way. The problem seems so big and unsolvable that we are tempted to close our eyes and hope it will go away but it won't. A wise person once spoke of the story of David and Goliath and said that when others looked at Goliath, they thought he was so big, you could never kill him. But when David looked at Goliath, he thought he was so big, you couldn't miss! We too must start looking at the problem of the homeless. It may be a big problem but it can never be solved until someone tries. To see how you could begin to help, see information in the bulletin today.

Sixteenth Sunday in Ordinary Time

Jeremiah 23:1-6
Ephesians 2:13-18
Mark 6:30-34

"Jesus saw a great crowd. He pitied them, for they were like sheep without a shepherd; and he began to teach them at great length."

Decoration

Make a sign that says FRIEND TO FRIEND—HELP FOR HELP, and place it in the center of your decoration. On one side, put schoolbooks, a child's lunchbox, a teen's tote bag—anything to indicate students. On the other side, put garden tools, a paintbrush, a weed trimmer, and maybe a box of trash bags or a snow shovel—anything to indicate chores to be done around the house. And, of course, a bit of greenery.

Celebration

Many children today seem to be like sheep without a shepherd; they need someone who has some time and love to share with them, someone who could give them a little extra help in one or more school subjects. At the same time, there are many retired senior citizens who would be great teachers but don't have as much energy as they once had to do chores around the house. Suggest a swap program today. Ask qualified seniors to volunteer to tutor students and ask students to pay for this help by doing simple chores. Appoint a contact person who would be willing to take phone calls and match up students to the person who would be best suited to teach them. If you have a parish school, ask the principal to post this idea on the bulletin board and to give you some names of students who might benefit. If the parish has an Over 50 Club, they may be willing to take on this project. Announce it in the bulletin today and see what develops!

Reflection

In today's gospel, Jesus sees a vast crowd—and pities them. Why does he pity them? Because they are poor or hungry or tired? No, because they are "like sheep without a shepherd," needing guidance. Jesus helps them by teaching. In our busy parish, there are also some who need help and maybe you can provide that help. Our altar decoration illustrates a new program we are beginning, Friend to Friend—Help for Help. Some of the young people in our parish may be good students but they need a little extra help in one particular subject, perhaps math or English or history or whatever. At the same time, there are some older members of our parish who know a lot about those subjects and would be great teachers but they might need help too—to get some chores done around the house. So if you need help or could give help, join this program today. It's free, and it can be fun too. If you're a student who hasn't been making good marks, here's your chance to improve them and at the same time, help somebody else. If you're an older parishioner who could generously share your knowledge with the younger generation, here's your chance. It can be fun to teach and fun to learn new things. Both the young people and the older people can benefit from this program and maybe make a new friend too! Check the bulletin for details.

Seventeenth Sunday in Ordinary Time

2 Kings 4:42-44
Ephesians 4:1-6
John 6:1-15

"Jesus then took the loaves of bread, gave thanks and passed them around....He did the same with the dried fish....When they had enough...they gathered twelve baskets full of pieces left over."

Decoration
Save your stale bread this week! Or go to a bakery and buy some day-old rolls on sale. Break them into pieces and pile them into three baskets to look like the plentiful leftovers of the crowd. Put greenery all around and add some vigil lights or luminaries.

Addition
Make one banner filled with the design of loaves of bread but make five of the loaves a different color or outline five in a bright color. Make a second banner filled with fish but again, make two of them a different color or outline them.

Celebration
If your parish has a hospitality committee or greeters, ask them to stand at the doors after all Masses, holding trays of small loaves of bread or muffins and offer them to the crowd as they leave. (You will have to get volunteers to buy or make these ahead of time. If you bake muffins in the smallest paper muffin cups, they will be easy to handle and you won't need so much batter.)

Reflection
The story of the loaves and fishes is one of the most popular in Scripture and familiar to most of us. We think first, of course, of the miracle. Then we notice that the apostles acted the same way we might have; they were skeptical about how much good those few loaves and fishes could do but finally, they did as Jesus asked. But what about the generosity of the little boy who gave

his loaves and fishes to feed the others? Unlike the apostles, he had no good reason to believe that Jesus could perform a miracle, no reason to share his food. But he did. He gave what little he had—and it was enough. As our decoration indicates, not only was it enough but there was plenty left over! Sometimes we hesitate to offer our help or give a small donation, thinking it too little to count. But when you give God whatever you have, no matter how little, it is always enough.

Eighteenth Sunday in Ordinary Time

Exodus 16:2-4, 12-15
Ephesians 4:17, 20-24
John 6:24-35

"You must no longer live as the pagans do—their minds empty." "I myself am the bread of life."

Decoration

Use a grouping today of all kinds of empty glass containers: clear glass vases, Mason jars, perfume bottles.... Add some pretty flowers and greenery or use a bright satiny cloth as a background that will set off the clear glass.

Celebration

Today you should suggest that people fill their minds with spiritual insights by reading religious books and magazines. Even if you have a spiritual lending library in the parish, some people like to have something they can take home and not have to worry about bringing it back, not have to worry if they want to cut out certain articles or highlight certain passages. But books and magazines are expensive to buy—so why not share! Put a box in the vestibule where people can leave any old spiritual books or magazines they don't want any more. Ask someone— maybe a teen group—to be responsible for sorting these. Arrange them in categories: Scripture, prayer, meditation, miscellaneous...and keep them available on a small table somewhere in the vestibule. Put up a sign: Spiritual Snacks, ten cents each. Selling them rather than giving them might make them seem more interesting, yet the ten cents price won't be too much for anyone to afford.

Reflection

"You must no longer live like pagans do—their minds empty." This interesting message from today's first reading is echoed in our decoration of empty containers to emphasize the fact that as Christians, we must not have empty minds but minds filled with a spiritual way of thinking. So how are we going to do that?

How are we going to fill our minds with things spiritual? One of the best ways is by reading good spiritual books and magazines—but that can get expensive! So let's share. Bring any religious books or magazines that you no longer want and leave them in the box in the vestibule. Our book chairperson will sort them out and display them and then you'll be able to browse and take some treasures home. We'll charge ten cents for each and if we make a little "bread," we'll use that to buy some books from a used book shop to add to the collection. The more you read about God, the more you learn. And the more you learn about someone, the easier it is to make friends.

NINETEENTH SUNDAY IN ORDINARY TIME

1 Kings 19:4-8
Ephesians 4:30-5:2
John 6:41-51

"I am the bread of life....If anyone eats this bread, he shall live forever."

Decoration

Go to the kitchen today! Gather up all the things you might use to make bread—a large mixing bowl, bag of flour, box of soda or baking powder (since a small cake of yeast wouldn't show up very well), a big wooden spoon, measuring spoons.... You could use a checkered kitchen tablecloth for a background and put some greenery in a crockery pitcher. Or make small placards, each with the name of a good quality—kindness, faith, chastity, patient endurance, love, mildness, generosity, joy, peacefulness. Hang these placards behind the altar.

Celebration

Before you read the reflection or before the homily or at the beginning or end of Mass, make a paper chain, the kind children make by cutting out strips of paper and gluing one together, then looping another into it and gluing that one together. Cut out large strips of paper and on each one, write one word in large letters, using the same words as those used in the altar decoration. Attach a piece of sturdy adhesive tape to the end of each one. Ask a group of parishioners to each carry one of these and come to the front of church. The first one should hold up the strip and read the word on it: KINDNESS. Then tape the strip together to form a loop. The second then reads on the next strip: FAITH, and then loops it into the first person's loop and tapes it together, and so on, until a long chain is formed. The chain can then be hung as a swag in front of or behind the altar (be sure to have hooks or some other way for it to be attached) or it could simply be put on the floor in front of today's decoration.

Reflection

A wise person once said that God provides for us all—even the birds of the air—but God does not put the food into each bird's nest! Just as the birds must fly about and search around to find what God has provided, we too must take the responsibility to search and find the proper ingredients for the bread of our daily life. In today's gospel, Jesus says, "I am the bread of life." Jesus has given us the eucharist, the true bread of life, but he has also given us free will to shape our individual daily lives. Our altar decoration shows the ingredients for making bread—flour, salt.... And the signs on the altar (chain) show us the ingredients needed to make a Christian life: kindness, faith, love, patient endurance, joy. If you have been too concerned with making a different kind of bread—money—think about trying another recipe. Try to receive the eucharist more frequently to experience that inner healing that can come only from Jesus, the bread of life. Try to stir into your life more qualities like patience and generosity so that you can make the daily bread of your life more Christian, more Christ-like.

Twentieth Sunday in Ordinary Time

Proverbs 9:1-6
Ephesians 5:15-20
John 6:51-58

"Be filled with the Spirit, addressing one another in psalms and hymns and inspired songs. Sing praise to the Lord with all your hearts."

Decoration

Make your decoration today using song sheets and opened hymnals. You might add some small musical instruments—a flute, a violin, a tambourine, and some greenery or flowers.

Addition

One or more banners depicting the message, "I will raise him up on the last day," perhaps rays coming from a cloud or a figure with outstretched arms rising into the clouds.

Celebration

Does your parish have a resurrection choir? If not, put a notice in the bulletin today asking for volunteers to form a choir/honor guard for funeral Masses. Make it clear that it is not necessary to have a choir-quality voice to join. Since funerals are often held on a weekday morning, music can be a problem because that's a difficult time for most choir members to attend. The resurrection choir is made up of anyone who can be available at that time of day, usually housewives, retirees, and possibly students in the summertime. They arrive early and wait in the vestibule for the funeral, then lead the procession down the aisle. They sit in the choir or in some other designated area of the church and sing along with the organist, providing mostly volume since funerals are often sparsely attended. At the end of the final blessing, they quietly go to the back of church and then come up the aisle, forming an honor guard on each side for the casket and mourners to pass through. The family is usually surprised and pleased by this honor or courtesy. (Since the parish Ladies Sodality and Men's Club or Knights of Columbus are good resources for this, you might ask that they announce it at their meetings in addition to your bulletin announcement. You will also need to have a contact person or a phone-chain to advise members of funeral times so you will have an adequate turnout.)

Reflection

Today's second reading tells us to address one another in psalms and hymns and inspired songs to sing praise to the Lord with all our hearts. Our altar decoration reminds us that "to sing is to praise twice" and we should all join our voices in song at all Masses. In addition, our choir is always ready to welcome new members so if there is anyone who would like to join, please contact the rectory or the organist. Or perhaps you could become a member of a different kind of choir, one that does not require you to sing well but to just show up! See the bulletin today for information about how to join our resurrection choir.

Twenty-First Sunday in Ordinary Time

Joshua 24:1-2, 15-17, 18
Ephesians 5:21-32
John 6:60-69

"Defer to one another out of reverence for Christ. Wives should be submissive to their husbands...husbands, love your wives....A man shall leave his father and mother, and shall cling to his wife, and the two shall be made one. This is a great foreshadowing; I mean that it refers to Christ and the church."

Decoration

Make a simple decoration today using one wedding candle with two single tapers, one on each side, to depict the marriage custom where the bride and groom each take a lighted candle and together use their individual candles to light one larger candle, symbolizing that they are to become one. You might add any kind of wedding decorations: white flowers, bows of white net, a white lace cloth for background....

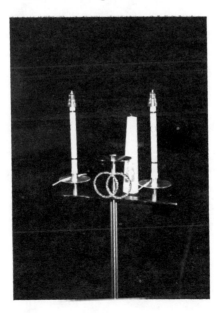

Addition

One banner with the wedding symbol of the cross with the two intertwined wedding rings; a second banner with two hands joined, a man's and a woman's, possibly showing wedding rings.

Celebration

Since the second reading addresses husbands and wives, perhaps this would be a good day to invite couples to renew marriage vows. You could ask them to stand or—since this might embarrass some—you could just ask them to remain seated and join hands as they repeat the vows after the priest. Or you could invite all those who are celebrating a decade or half-decade anniversary—10, 20, 30... or 5, 10, 15, 20...to sit in front pews and then stand and renew vows. Or you could have coffee and donuts after Mass to honor all newlyweds, couples who have been married within the past year. (This might also be a good opportunity to tell them about parish organizations and encourage them to get involved in parish activities!)

Reflection

The decoration today draws our attention to the second reading, which tells wives that the husband is head of his wife just as Christ is head of his body, the church. And it reminds husbands to love their wives as Christ loved the church. The wedding symbolism is so often tied to Christ and the church. Perhaps we should remember this as we listen to today's gospel reading where Jesus' disciples are murmuring in protest and finally break away and refuse to remain in his company any more. In a time when our country and our church are so beset with the painful problems of divorce, let us pray especially this week for all couples who are having marriage problems and for a renewal to the lifelong commitment that "two shall be made one."

Twenty-Second Sunday in Ordinary Time

Deuteronomy 4:1-2, 6-8
James 1:17-18, 21-22, 27
Mark 7:1-8, 14-15, 21-23

"Why do your disciples not follow the tradition of our ancestors, but instead take food without purifying their hands?"
"This people pays me lip service but their heart is far from me."

Decoration
Let your decoration today depict purity. Use a white cloth, white flowers, a clear bowl of water or an antique pitcher and bowl (the kind that great-grandma had in the bedroom to use when washing the hands and face). Place several folded white handtowels on one side and have a small glass bowl filled with small bars of soap on the other side.

Celebration
Perhaps you could have someone cut out lots of hearts—in various colors of construction paper—and put them in small baskets. Then, after today's reflection is read, children could come up and take the baskets and pass out hearts to all. Or you could put a drawing of a heart in the bulletin with these words from the gospel, "This people pays me lip service but their heart is far from me." Inside the drawing of the heart, put these words, WHERE IS YOUR HEART?

Reflection
Our decoration today reflects the gospel story where the Pharisees are criticizing Jesus' disciples because they have not always followed the tradition of purifying themselves—or washing their hands—before meals. Jesus calls the Pharisees hypocrites and speaks of those whose reverence is empty because they disregard God's commandments and cling to human tradition...because they pay lip service when their heart is far from

God. In today's world, many people carefully follow society's rules for good conduct, washing their hands in public, being careful to always make a good appearance in business and in social circles and perhaps also in their religion. But is their reverence empty because they are only paying lip service while they disregard God's commandments, never fully accepting the Christian way of life in their hearts, never completely surrendering to God's will? What about you? Look into your heart today. Does God come first there? Or have you been only paying lip service?

TWENTY-THIRD SUNDAY IN ORDINARY TIME

Isaiah 35:4-7
James 2:1-5
Mark 7:31-37

"Some people brought him a deaf man who had a speech impediment and begged him to lay his hand on him."

Decoration

Try something really different today! Make an arrangement of artificial greenery or real greenery that won't wilt—like ivy. Then just take some sheets of tissue paper—in several different colors—and crumple each sheet. Place these crumpled pieces in among the greenery (to illustrate that there are a variety of ways in which people can become physically crumpled).

Celebration

Since deafness is an invisible handicap, there may be deaf or hearing-impaired parishioners who feel left out of the faith community. Today, ask someone who knows sign language to come and "sign" the gospel, or perhaps sign the entire Mass. Then, make an effort to discover if there is a need in your parish to help the hearing-impaired. Put a questionnaire in the bulletin to this effect:

We want to help hearing-impaired parishioners hear the good news and participate more fully in parish activities. Please fill this out and return it to the rectory or drop it in the collection basket next week.

_____ I have a hearing problem.

I find it difficult to hear ___ the homily; ___ the readings; ___ the priest in the confessional.

If installed, I would use a hearing aid in the confessional ___ yes ___ no; and/or a hearing aid in a side pew during Mass ___ yes___ no. Here's a suggestion that would help hearing-impaired parishioners:_____ .

If you wish to be contacted about this problem, please add your name and address or phone—or—if you wish, you may remain anonymous.

Name_____

Address _____ or Phone_____

Depending on how many responses you get, you may wish to consider starting some kind of parish ministry for those with hearing difficulty.

Reflection

Since today's gospel focuses on the story of a deaf man, our crumpled altar decoration is a reminder that there are many ways in which people can become physically crumpled. All too often we overlook the problems of the hearing-impaired because this is an invisible handicap. You can't help but notice someone who is blind or in a wheel chair and you are moved to reach out to help them. But someone with a hearing difficulty also has a great cross to bear because it becomes so difficult to communicate, to share, to participate in family or parish activities. Perhaps we have overlooked this problem in our parish and we would like your help in addressing it. If you or someone you know has a hearing problem that makes it difficult to hear the homilies or go to confession or hear the speakers at parish gatherings, please fill out the questionaire in today's bulletin and let us know how we can help. And for those of you who do not have a hearing problem, this week think about how well you hear the homily, the readings, the prayers. How often do you listen—but hear not?

Twenty-Fourth Sunday in Ordinary Time

Isaiah 50:4-9
James 2:14-18
Mark 8:27-35

"If a man wishes to come after me, he must deny his very self, take up his cross, and follow in my steps."

Decoration

If your parish has any kind of relics, display them today. (Often they are contained in a case that would make an attractive display but if not, ask your pastor for advice about how best to display them correctly. Perhaps you could use a velvet background and put them in a gold shadowbox.) Add vigil lights and flowers and put an incense burner at each side of the display. If you do not have any relics, use pictures of saints. Put them in pretty frames and again, add the vigil lights, flowers, and incense burners.

Celebration

Today's Christians should do as the saints did—follow in Jesus' footsteps, not just on Sunday but every day. And, since so many Christians are working today, there has been a recent up-surge of organizations of Christian businessmen and women with the goal of bringing Christianity into the workplace and ex-panding the understanding of the spirituality of work. If there is such a group in your city, ask a representative to speak today and invite parishioners to join. If not, put a notice in the bulletin asking if anyone would be interested in forming such a group in your own parish or in trying to organize an ecumenical group in your area, with the hope of expanding it eventually into a city-wide group.

Reflection

The focus of today's decoration is relics (saints' pictures) to honor and memorialize those who truly obeyed Jesus' command in today's gospel to "follow in his steps." We sometimes think that saints existed only in the past, only in stories of long, long ago. But there are many saints in our world today. And Jesus ex-pects many more. He asks us all to be saints, to follow in his foot-steps. That sometimes seems especially difficult in today's world when so many people spend most of their days in work places far removed from spiritual surroundings. So what can you do? You can bring Christianity into the workplace and give a full day's work for a full day's pay, show social justice to all you en-counter in everyday situations, become aware that the circle of your life connects work with faith, family, and community. Even if your work is boring or difficult, you can make it meaningful by being grateful that you have work to do and by welcoming God as a co-worker in your everyday life. See the bulletin today for information about joining (forming) a group of Christian working men and women.

Twenty-Fifth Sunday in Ordinary Time

Wisdom 2:12, 17-20
James 3:16-4:3
Mark 9:30-37

"If anyone wishes to rank first, he must remain the last one of all and the servant of all....Whoever welcomes a child such as this for my sake welcomes me."

Decoration
Make a decoration today of "childish" things—dolls, toys, baby rattles, baby shoes, stuffed animals....Perhaps use some baby bottles as candleholders and add some flowers or greenery.

Addition
Cut out some paper dolls! You know how children fold paper and then cut out stick men so that when the paper unfolds, they have a row of stick people holding hands? Use a long row of these today across the edge of the altar or an even longer row all across the wall behind the altar. Or make posters using the design of stick people holding hands.

Celebration
Does your parish have a preschool religion program or baby-sitting during one of the Masses or a Mother's Day Out program? If so, ask today for volunteers to help with this work. If volunteers can't give time, perhaps they could donate cookies, storybooks, coloring books, small blankets for naptime, or whatever items the programs need. If you don't have such programs, you might like to consider starting one or more and announce the fact in today's bulletin. (The Mother's Day Out has volunteers who will come to the church and babysit for several hours while mothers go shopping or run errands or gather together for a fun-program with a carryout lunch from a fast-food restaurant. If this kind of program is not possible, you could organize a baby-sitting co-op where mothers take turns caring for each other's children in order to earn free time away from home.)

Reflection

In today's gospel, once again we see the disciples behaving as we ourselves often do. They are embarrassed when Jesus finds out they've been arguing about who is the most important! Do you sometimes feel embarrassed when you suddenly realize that God has heard what you just said or God has seen you arguing or trying to act important? Our altar decoration of people holding hands reminds us that Jesus tells his disciples the first should be willing to rank last and to be the servant of all. We must all be equal, holding hands, ready to help each other. Jesus also tells his friends, "Whoever welcomes a little child for my sake welcomes me." See the bulletin today for ways to help the children in our parish. Then look around at your own family, your own neighborhood. Do you take the children for granted? Or do you welcome them? Resolve today to reach out more: to the children in your parish, in your neighborhood, and in your own family.

TWENTY-SIXTH SUNDAY IN ORDINARY TIME

Numbers 11, 25-29
James 5:1-6
Mark 9:38-43, 45, 47-48

"Teacher, we saw a man using your name to expel demons and we tried to stop him because he is not of our company." "Do not try to stop him....Anyone who is not against us is with us."

Decoration
The focal point of today's decoration can be one thing: a stop sign! You probably can't borrow one from the highway department but you might find a cardboard one in a party supply store. Or maybe you could get one from a school-crossing guard or make a sign, using bright red paint on white cardboard. As usual, flank with flowers or greenery and candles.

Celebration
Perhaps you could issue an invitation in the bulletin today to an ecumenical gathering. Invite members of neighboring non-Catholic churches to join your parishioners for a potluck supper provided by the ladies of the parish or meet in a private meeting room at a neighborhood restaurant for dinner. Invite someone to speak on a scriptural topic that would be appropriate for all and spend a social evening.

Reflection
In today's first reading, a young man asks Moses to stop others who are prophesying but Moses responds that he wishes "all people of the Lord were prophets!" In the gospel, a similar scene occurs when the disciples want to stop a man who is using Jesus' name to dispel demons. But Jesus says, "Who is not against us is with us." Our altar decoration reminds us that we often want to

stop others who are not exactly like us, because we are jealous or afraid of or prejudiced against those who are of a different race or religion or even different backgrounds or social strata. In another part of the gospel, Jesus tells us that if a hand or foot or eye offends, we should get rid of it. If we have a bad habit, we should stop it. What is your offense? Is it perhaps prejudice? Is that one of the things you should get rid of, should stop? Please notice the invitation in the bulletin today to an ecumenical gathering, an evening of fellowship with neighboring Christians.

Twenty-Seventh Sunday in Ordinary Time

Genesis 2:18-24
Hebrews 2:9-11
Mark 10:2-16 or 10, 2-12

"Let no man separate what God has joined."

Decoration
Today get one of those cardboard sunscreens that are used to put behind the windshield of a car in the summer to keep heat off the steering wheel and front seat. Find one that has a pleasant design that would be appropriate for a display. All you will need to add is a fern or large potted plant on each side of the sunscreen.

Celebration
Try to find a current, worthwhile article about the sanctity of marriage or the problems modern married couples face and ways to handle them—something that suggests seeing possibilities rather than problems and alternatives to hurrying into a divorce. Make copies of this and use it as a bulletin insert or pass it out at the door or leave it in the pews.

Reflection
Although in today's gospel Jesus tells us that in marriage man and woman become one and no one should separate what God has joined, divorce has become a reality of modern life. It is a deep sadness in today's society and in today's Catholic church, and a special sadness for children of divorce. In some cases, divorce is the only possible solution but it seems that it is sometimes chosen as a quick solution to problems that might be worked out. And perhaps that is true of many other areas of Christian life as well; we take the easy way rather than the difficult way of lifelong commitment. Our altar decoration reminds

us to stop screening out possibilities for solutions to problems, to stop hiding behind hurts, to throw away the protective shield that helps us forget commitments and responsibilities. Remember, there are few bargains in life. Success in business is bought with hard work. Success in relationships is bought with self-denial and generosity as well as love. Success in life is bought with Christian commitment. If you are shirking some commitment, don't screen out God. Open yourself to God's help. Place your hope in God.

TWENTY-EIGHTH SUNDAY IN ORDINARY TIME

Wisdom 7:7-11
Hebrews 4:12-13
Mark 10:17-30 or 10, 17-27

"God's word is living and effective, sharper than any two-edged sword." "Then who can be saved?" "For man it is impossible but not for God. With God all things are possible."

Decoration

Time for some detective work! Ask about the parish and try to find someone who has a decorative sword—perhaps one that hangs on a wall or is displayed on a stand or in a case. Borrow it for today's decoration, and that's all you will need. Or if you can't find one like this, use a child's toy sword but add some greenery or flowers to make it look more interesting. To help it show up better, you might use two fancy plate stands that are used to display decorative plates. Put one at each end of the sword to prop it up so that it can be displayed horizontally.

Celebration

Suggest in the bulletin or with an announcement that each person choose just one or two lines from today's readings or go later to the Bible and thumb through it and randomly pick out one short passage. Let this message be the living word and meditate on it for a few minutes each day this week.

Reflection

"Who can be saved?" In today's gospel, the disciples are troubled. The rich man has followed God's commandments but Jesus says that is not enough. Perhaps he is telling us that the commandments are the minimum for anyone to live a decent life—to not kill or steal or lie or hurt others. But is this enough for Jesus' followers, for real Christians? Shouldn't they want to do more than the minimum? The disciples wonder how anyone can do enough to earn salvation. Jesus fixes his gaze on them and says, "For man it is impossible but not for God. With God all things are possible"—*with God.* How can we be with God? The second reading tells us that God's word is living and effective, sharper than any two-edged sword. Our altar decoration reminds us to look to the sword, to the word, to the living word of Scripture. When we try to live by the word, we are with God. And with God, all things are possible.

Twenty-Ninth Sunday in Ordinary Time

Isaiah 53:10-11
Hebrews 4:14-16
Mark 10:35-45 or 10, 42-45

"Jesus called [the Twelve] together and said to them: 'You know how among the Gentiles those who seem to exercise authority lord it over them; their great ones make their importance felt. It cannot be like that with you."

Decoration

Find a large picture of Da Vinci's painting of the *Last Supper* and use this as the central decoration. Flank it on each side with greenery and possibly gold candlesticks holding lighted candles.

Celebration

Perhaps you could give out holy cards today with a picture of the Last Supper. Or you could reproduce the picture in the bulletin with a shortened version of the Da Vinci story in today's reflection.

Reflection

In today's gospel, Jesus has called the twelve apostles together and is telling them that they should not lord it over others; they should not try to make their importance felt. They should follow his example and not come to be served but to serve. Our altar decoration shows Jesus with his apostles and is a reminder of a story about this painting. When Leonardo da Vinci decided to paint the *Last Supper*, he poured all his energy into the project, working early and late. He read and reread the pages of the Bible, pondering every word, trying to depict the scene as perfectly as possible. At last he was finished! Satisfied with his work, he invited a few of his friends to come in and see it. They looked at his masterpiece and marveled at it. Then one of them commented that the glowing, golden chalice was the most beautiful object in the picture. Da Vinci immediately snatched up his brush, dipped it in black paint and smeared it on the canvas, painting out the chalice. Then he turned to his friend and said, "If what you tell me is true, my painting is a failure. I meant my master's face to be the most beautiful object in the painting." The great artist did not want to show his own importance in painting a masterpiece; he wanted his artistry to draw others to look at Jesus, to see Jesus first. Remember this week to look away from yourself and toward Jesus.

THIRTIETH SUNDAY IN ORDINARY TIME

Jeremiah 31:7-9
Hebrews 5:1-6
Mark 10:46-52

"You are a priest forever, according to the order of Melchizedek."

Decoration
Ask the pastor and assistants if they have any photographs of their ordination that you could borrow. If not, try to borrow ordination pictures of the most recently ordained priests in your city. If all else fails, just use any photographs of young priests. Add white flowers, white vigil lights, and perhaps some colorful stoles.

Addition
If your parish has school or CCD classes, ask one or more classes to have a vocation poster contest and hang all—or only the winning posters—instead of banners.

Celebration
Invite several people to make brief talks about priestly vocations today. Perhaps you could ask a small boy to speak about what he thinks a priest does and why anyone would want to be one...followed by a teenager giving his ideas about vocations...followed by the parent of a priest speaking about a son's experience...followed by the pastor or associate telling of his own priestly calling.

Reflection
Today's decoration reflects the words in the second reading: "Every high priest is taken from among men and made their representative before God...one does not take this honor on his own initiative, but only when called by God." Today we have invited several people to give you their own interpretation of this call from God to the life of a priest, a priest forever by the order of Melchizedek.

111

THIRTY-FIRST SUNDAY IN ORDINARY TIME

Deuteronomy 6:2-6
Hebrews 7:23-28
Mark 12:28-34

"This is the first [commandment]...you shall love the Lord your God with all your heart, with all your soul, with all your mind, and with all your strength. This is the second, you shall love your neighbor as yourself."

Decoration

Cut out large silhouettes of different groups of people, two men or two women talking to each other, a father and son or daughter, a group of teenagers, a child on a tricycle talking with an older child, a family of mother-child-father.... Cut these from brightly colored cardboard and attach them to the walls all around the church to illustrate neighbors. (You can find stencils of silhouettes and then enlarge them to use as your patterns.) Depending on the architecture of your church, you might want to use twisted crepe paper streamers to go from one silhouette to the next, indicating a joining. Or if this is not possible, you could simply make banners with silhouettes of different people: children, adults, teens, senior citizens—in groups or alone.

Addition
You could add flowers or greenery in front of the altar, or perhaps a picnic basket with lots of flowers spilling out of it.

Celebration
Perhaps you could ask everyone to a picnic this (Sunday) afternoon as a way to get to know their neighbors better. As part of the festivity, plan to have a tree planting! Select an appropriate spot and purchase a small to medium-size tree (depending on what your budget allows!). Have the hole dug ahead of time and ready for planting. Let everyone gather around while the pastor blesses the tree and sprinkles it with holy water. Then, once the tree is in position, everyone could take turns adding shovelfuls of dirt, so each person present can say he or she planted a tree that day! Then have someone ready with a camera and take photos of family groups or neighbor groups with the tree. Perhaps this could become an annual picnic with the same groups trying to re-assemble to have more pictures taken to show that the tree has grown and the children in the families too!

Reflection
Just two commandments: love God and love your neighbor. That should be easy enough, shouldn't it? But, of course, we all know that it isn't. Our decorations today depict neighbors of all kinds. We neighbors have all come together today to worship as a community and to show our love for God. Now we invite all our parish family to get to know your neighbors better by coming together this (Sunday) afternoon for a parish picnic and a tree planting! Planting a tree together symbolizes a new beginning and the promise of growth. And as we think about the commandment to love your neighbor, we might remember the giant sequoia tree. A tree so large might be expected to have very deep roots. Instead, the roots are fairly shallow. But the roots of each sequoia intermingle with the roots of other sequoias, each giving the other strength. Alone, each tree would topple, but together, interlocked, they hold each other up. That's how we should love our neighbor, each helping the other, each depending on the other, each holding the other up, safe from the winds and storms of everyday life.

This (Sunday) afternoon, bring a picnic lunch and plant a tree with your neighbors. See the bulletin for details.

THIRTY-SECOND SUNDAY IN ORDINARY TIME

1 Kings 17, 10:16
Hebrews 9:24-28
Mark 12:38-44 or 12:41-44

"One poor widow came and put in two small copper coins worth about a cent."

Decoration
Use several clear glass containers—tall, short, round, square....Fill each with lots of shiny copper pennies. Plus, of course, the usual greenery and possibly some orange or yellow votive lights.

Celebration
Ask people to start saving pennies for the missions, and have a container in some safe place each Sunday where people can deposit them. Put a label on the container: For the Missions—Pennies Make Good Cents. Choose one particular mission so you can tell the people where their donations are going. To get it started today, you might get penny-wrappers from the bank and give them out after Mass to anyone who wants one.

Reflection
What can a penny buy today? Not much you'll say. But maybe that's not quite right. In today's gospel, the poor widow gave two copper coins—not much, but all she had. Today's copper coins seem to have become almost worthless and are a lot of trouble to carry around. People are always trying to get rid of all the pennies in pocket or purse. Well, here's a good way to do that. Find a container, perhaps similar to the ones in today's decoration, and start to fill it with your loose pennies. If every family saved just a few pennies each day, it would soon mount into a few dollars and this would be enough to buy food for maybe a day or a week or even a year for some poor person living in a poverty-stricken country. Bring your pennies to church each Sunday and leave them in the collection box that will be located

at _____ . All pennies collected will be sent to _____ Mission. This is a project in which all parishioners, from children to senior citizens, can participate. We don't ask that you give a lot of pennies—just all that you have! Like the poor widow. And to get you started, we are giving out penny-wrappers from the bank. But don't think you'll have to wrap all your pennies. This is just a reminder to save your copper coins for the missions because saving pennies makes good cents!

Thirty-Third Sunday in Ordinary Time

Daniel 12:1-3
Hebrews 10:11-14, 18
Mark 13:24-32

"...the sun will be darkened, the moon will not shed its light, stars will fall out of the skies...then men will see the Son of Man coming in the clouds with great power and glory."

Decoration

Perhaps the best decoration for today would simply be two banners. One should be made of black velvet or felt with just a tiny bit of a golden sun showing at the upper edge and silver stars falling toward the bottom edge. The other banner should be made of bright shiny yellow satin with white poufy clouds and rays of golden sequins glittering. If you can locate an ornamental miniature fig tree, you could simply place this in front of or to the side of the altar.

Celebration

Reproduce today's responsorial psalm: "Keep me safe, O God; you are my hope," on small sheets of paper and distribute them to be taken home.

Reflection

Today's gospel reading is a sombre but glorious one. As our banners depict, it foretells a time when the sun will be darkened, the moon will not shed its light and the stars will fall out of the skies. But then—after the darkness—the Son of Man will come in power and glory. The Lord never gives us darkness without a bright glimmer of hope and salvation. If you are going through a dark time in your life, give up the pain, give up the darkness. Turn it all over to God and trust in his power and glory. This week, remember today's responsorial psalm which is both a prayer and a promise. "Keep me safe, O God; you are my hope."

LAST SUNDAY IN ORDINARY TIME
Our Lord Jesus Christ, Universal King

Daniel 7:13-14
Revelation 1:5-8
John 18:33-37

"My kingdom does not belong to this world...."

Decoration

Take a long pole (perhaps a broom stick) and attach a crossbar to the top of it. If the pole you use is new, leave as is but if it looks a bit shabby, just wrap pole and crossbar in white ribbon. Then take strips of ribbon of different colors—red, yellow, orange, blue, tan, pink—and cut them in different lengths. Sew a small bell on the end of each ribbon (possibly a jingle bell from last Christmas). Attach the multi-colored ribbons all across the top crossbar so they will hang down and swing and the bells will jingle as they move. If possible, make two of these poles so that they can be carried in the entrance procession, jingling merrily to announce the coming of a King, then place one at each side of the altar. If you only have one pole, place it in a prominent place, in front of but to the side of the altar so it will not obstruct the view of the altar. Have some sort of holder—possibly a candle-stand—where the pole(s) can be secured and stand up straight. In front of the altar, make a royal arrangement of golden flowers and sprinkle glitter on the blossoms or make bows of gold foil

and put these in with the flowers or possibly drape some strands of gold beads amid or around the flowers.

Addition

One banner with the design of a golden crown and the symbols for Alpha and Omega. Another banner made with colorful sequins in the design of fireworks.

Celebration

Perhaps you could suggest that the king's subjects petition for favors on this special feast. Make a box labeled Prayer Petitions and put a small pad of paper and some pencils next to it. If your church has a statue of Christ the King, place it at the foot of the statue. If not, put it by a side altar.

Reflection

Today we celebrate the glorious feast of Christ the King, a king whose kingdom is not of this world, a king who is our ruler but also our friend. In ancient kingdoms, a special feast day was often an occasion when the king's subjects were invited to ask for a special favor to be granted. Perhaps you too have a special favor you would like granted by your king. We have placed a prayer petition box at_____ and we invite you to write down your request and put it in the box. Since Jesus spoke of "when two or more are gathered together in my name," we will place the petition box near the altar during every Mass this week and pray as a community for your intentions. We also suggest that each of you might like to say one extra prayer every day this week, storming heaven, asking God to grant the petitions that have been placed in the box. Perhaps our combined prayers will be like incense rising in celebration of this royal feast of Christ the King. If your petition is granted, please tell the pastor so we can celebrate with you. Just remember: God always answers prayers, but sometimes the answer is no. So don't be disappointed if your petition is not granted. Maybe it is not time yet or maybe God has different plans for you. Sometimes you think you know what you need but God knows better because he can see around the corners and you can't. Bow to his will, acknowledge his majesty, and you will be richly rewarded with his love. Christ the King is the Alpha and the Omega, the one who is and who was and who is to come. And he is also your friend.